NEW DIRECTIONS FOR ADULT AND CONTINUING EDUCATION

Ralph G. Brockett, *University of Tennessee, Knoxville*
EDITOR-IN-CHIEF

Alan B. Knox, *University of Wisconsin, Madison*
CONSULTING EDITOR

Learning Environments for Women's Adult Development: Bridges Toward Change

Kathleen Taylor
Saint Mary's College of California

Catherine Marienau
DePaul University

EDITORS

Number 65, Spring 1995

JOSSEY-BASS PUBLISHERS
San Francisco

LEARNING ENVIRONMENTS FOR WOMEN'S ADULT DEVELOPMENT:
BRIDGES TOWARD CHANGE
Kathleen Taylor, Catherine Marienau (eds.)
New Directions for Adult and Continuing Education, no. 65
Ralph G. Brockett, Editor-in-Chief
Alan B. Knox, Consulting Editor

LC 85-644750   ISSN 0195-2242   ISBN 0-7879-9911-3

NEW DIRECTIONS FOR ADULT AND CONTINUING EDUCATION is part of The Jossey-Bass Higher and Adult Education Series and is published quarterly by Jossey-Bass Inc., Publishers, 350 Sansome Street, San Francisco, California 94104-1342 (publication number USPS 493-930). Second-class postage paid at San Francisco, California, and at additional mailing offices. POSTMASTER: Send address changes to New Directions for Adult and Continuing Education, Jossey-Bass Inc., Publishers, 350 Sansome Street, San Francisco, California 94104-1342.

SUBSCRIPTIONS for 1995 cost $48.00 for individuals and $64.00 for institutions, agencies, and libraries.

EDITORIAL CORRESPONDENCE should be sent to the Editor-in-Chief, Ralph G. Brockett, Department of Educational Leadership, University of Tennessee, 239 Claxton Addition, Knoxville, Tennessee 37996-3400.

Cover photograph by Wernher Krutein/PHOTOVAULT © 1990.

Manufactured in the United States of America. Nearly all Jossey-Bass books, jackets, and periodicals are printed on recycled paper that contains at least 50 percent recycled waste, including 10 percent postconsumer waste. Many of our materials are also printed with vegetable-based inks; during the printing process, these inks emit fewer volatile organic compounds (VOCs) than petroleum-based inks. VOCs contribute to the formation of smog.

Contents

EDITORS' NOTES

For years after the educational reforms of the 1970s gave rise to alternative, adult, and degree-completion programs, many of us who work with reentry women in such settings found ourselves informally sharing information and insights. Our discoveries, questions, and concerns were out of the educational mainstream and were not well represented in the literature. The issues that concerned us were twice-removed from those that our colleagues in more traditional programs faced: first, because our focus was on nontraditional students (that is, an older and highly diverse population)—an increasingly numerous but often semidisenfranchised group on many campuses—and second, because our focus was women's issues, whereas much of the literature on learning and development was male-oriented.

More recently, a growing body of literature on adult development and feminist pedagogy has begun to illuminate issues that had previously been relegated to "corridor talk." This research on women's epistemology, learning styles, educational needs, and psychosocial and psychological development suggests that historical and current educational norms and approaches may not serve men and women equally.

The central aim of this sourcebook is to help make learning environments more supportive of reentry women in their ongoing development. We (the editors) showcase certain educational practices that tend to be based in alternative adult higher education settings. These practices emerged from the challenges of meeting the needs of diverse women learners. The development theories we focus on are those that specifically embrace women, both as learners and as developing adults. Our intent is to link theory and practice in ways that speak directly to the concerns of educators serving diverse populations of adult learners, particularly women.

While this book focuses specifically on women's learning and development, we believe that the innovative new practices and recent theories explored in this volume are likely to serve both men and women better than do traditional approaches. We do not suggest practices that ask educators to choose who should be better served.

Over the last twenty-five years, we have intuitively linked adult learning, adult development, women's development, and feminist pedagogy while working in the context of alternative higher education for adults. This book grows out of our attempts to articulate the links between our experiences and the emerging literature in these areas. What pulls together the various pedagogical approaches presented in this volume is that they all provide ways of helping a woman learner shape the narrative of her evolving self in her multiple life contexts. Each approach affirms the central roles of self and experience in learning that lead to development.

The authors in this volume explore and elucidate these links from a variety of perspectives. They teach in adult-centered programs in community colleges, state colleges, and private universities; they are administrators, program directors, faculty members, and mentors. Some of them were reentry women learners themselves. All of them have worked extensively with women (and most of them with men) who did not complete college at the "regular" age and who reentered or started college in programs designed specifically for adults.

The first chapter sets the stage by providing a brief retrospective on various strands of practice and inquiry that are leading toward more supportive learning environments for adults. It also introduces two especially salient theoretical constructs to help educators understand the effectiveness of current approaches and practices and to inform improvements and directions for the future.

The next four chapters focus on helping women learners gain greater awareness of themselves as knowers and as developing individuals. Chapter Two describes, in practical terms, how a structured learning journal helps women learners develop as knowers. Self-assessment, as it is described in Chapter Three, can be considered a particular approach to journal writing (or vice versa), as well as a comprehensive strategy for helping women learners make more complex meaning from their experience. Chapter Four emphasizes the self-reflective component in the assessment of prior learning, as a way not only to validate a woman's experience but also to further develop her own authentic way of knowing. In Chapter Five, women learners describe how learning about women's development in general stimulates their own individual development, a process that is influenced in part by including their own voices and experiences as course content.

Chapter Six explores the significance of the diverse voices that reentry women represent and considers how teaching strategies that work well with most mainstream reentry women may need to be adapted for women of color and nonnative English speakers. Chapter Seven moves beyond individual strategies to describe an entire curriculum explicitly constructed to further women's development. Drawing on the research and theoretical work of Belenky, Clinchy, Goldberger, and Tarule (1986), Ursuline College has created a new core curriculum that attempts to provide developmental steppingstones for reentry women. Mentoring, of the kind described in Chapter Eight, supports the developmental process of a woman learner through a relationship with a faculty mentor that is fluid and elastic in response to her needs.

Chapter Nine examines the relationships among learning, teaching, and development that lead to learning-centered teaching strategies; these strategies help women develop authentic voices and ways of knowing that they can apply in their daily lives. Chapter Ten examines Kegan's (1994) model of orders of consciousness and complexity of mind, and it considers how the kinds of educational approaches and strategies presented in this volume can help adult learners develop their capabilities for successfully meeting the demands of modern life.

We wish to acknowledge the colleagues who generously read and responded to all or portions of this manuscript, sometimes when they were busily engaged in projects of their own: Carrie Bassett, Richard Haswell, Robert Kegan, Jean MacGregor, Rebecca Proehl, Don Stone. Our contributing authors also read and commented on one another's works, and we extend special thanks to Phyllis Walden. In addition, Morris Fiddler examined multiple drafts of every chapter; his ability to think critically and appreciatively contributed to the conceptual clarity of our own thinking and writing. And most especially, we wish to appreciate and acknowledge the hundreds of women learners with whom we have worked and learned, whose experiences inform this book. Most of the quotations from these learners come from three sources: Taylor's previous research (1991), informal interviews conducted by the chapter authors with students and other teachers and mentors, and the journals and self-assessments of learners in each author's own institution. Though we have occasionally and minimally edited their words for the sake of clarity, these women learners' voices are the powerful core around which this volume turns.

Though it is not customary to dedicate a volume such as this, we wish to take special note of the women whose ongoing development we most cherish, our daughters Anna Dinaburg, Rebekkah Dinaburg, Anna Marienau Roth, and Alissa Stolz.

Catherine Marienau
Kathleen Taylor
Editors

References

Belenky, M. F., Clinchy, B. M., Goldberger, N. R., and Tarule, J. M. *Women's Ways of Knowing: The Development of Self, Voice, and Mind.* New York: Basic Books, 1986.

Kegan, R. *In Over Our Heads: The Mental Demands of Modern Life.* Cambridge, Mass.: Harvard University Press, 1994.

Taylor, K. "Transforming Learning: Experiences of Adult Development and Transformation of Re-entry Learners in an Adult Degree Program." Unpublished doctoral dissertation, Union Graduate School, The Union Institute, 1991.

CATHERINE MARIENAU *is associate professor in the School for New Learning at DePaul University and is active in the Alliance (an association for alternative degree programs for adults). She has worked in alternative higher education for adults for over twenty years, serving as teacher, adviser, mentor, program developer and administrator, researcher, writer, and consultant.*

KATHLEEN TAYLOR *is associate professor at Saint Mary's College of California, chair of the Department of Portfolio Instruction, and a consultant on women's development and education. She returned to college to complete her bachelor's degree twenty years after starting it.*

Three strands of practice and inquiry—adult learning, women's development, and feminist pedagogy—come together in the context of alternative higher education for adults to help attune learning environments to women's developmental needs.

Bridging Practice and Theory for Women's Adult Development

Kathleen Taylor, Catherine Marienau

Barbara is forty-two years old, Caucasian, and single.

> When I told my parents I wanted to get a degree in nursing, my father told me I didn't need that much education; so I got a three-year diploma instead. It took me years to realize that I would not be betraying my parents if I completed more education than they had.

Betty is sixty-two, Caucasian, and married.

> I worked while my husband got his master's degree, and I helped put all five of my children through college. Now it's my turn.

Burdette is thirty-seven, Caucasian, and married.

> I married right after high school and had two kids before I was twenty-one. Then, with my husband in the navy and out at sea eight months every year, it was all I could do to raise the family, mostly by myself. When my kids got older, I went to work, but the jobs I qualified for weren't challenging and didn't pay much.

Esther is forty-nine, African American, and married.

> I started college right out of high school but quit in my first year to marry and have a family. I'm still married, have three wonderful children, and have held challenging jobs in both the private and nonprofit sectors. But I am still plagued

by the unfinished business of my degree. I'm not even sure what I will do with it. I just know that getting and finishing my education is about me—Esther.

Maria is twenty-eight, Latina, and divorced.

I am the first woman in my family to get a divorce and the first to pursue a college education—I don't know which is harder for my mother to accept. What I know is that I must step outside the boundaries of my culture and learn to make my own way in the world. I need an education to do that.

Penny is twenty-five, Caucasian, and separated.

Some people would say my parents were abusive; they just raised us the way they were raised. I grew up thinking I was stupid. It never occurred to me to think about college. But when my daughter was tested as "gifted," I knew I had to do something so she wouldn't think I was a dope.

These are a few of the voices among the growing number of adult women undergraduates. Women now account for more than 52 percent of an increasingly diverse college population (Maher and Tetreault, 1994, p. 2), and nearly half again as many women as men in college today are between the ages of twenty-five and forty-nine ("College Enrollment by Age of Students, Fall 1992," 1994, p. 15).

An Inhospitable Climate

If asked why they are in college, most adult women initially talk about what a college degree will do for them in the marketplace. They want to change jobs, would like more fulfilling careers, are ready for new responsibilities, need better pay. But in time, other reasons emerge—sometimes boldly, sometimes hesitantly, as if naming their hopes might break an enchantment. They speak of "becoming someone" or of "finding out who I am." For all these women, education represents change—a major shift in how they have lived their lives and, at a more basic level, who they have been and who they might become in the future.

It is hardly surprising, then, that these women enter institutions of higher education with some trepidation. "Can I really do this?" they wonder. Or, "Do I really deserve doing all this for *me*?" Women are plagued by these questions despite their abilities, their often impressive professional accomplishments, and their evident enthusiasm. If we educators are aware of a woman's anxiety and apprehension (and she does not always let us know), we may see her as lacking in self-confidence or self-esteem. "How absurd," we may say to ourselves (and if we are insensitive, to the woman herself). We say, "Look at all you've accomplished to get here." We try to acknowledge her efforts, validate her successes, and offer her suggestions for improvements; and we assume she will come to believe in herself. But it can be difficult for her to do that—believe in herself, act for herself, speak up for herself—in the face of an often inhospitable learning environment.

The barriers that returning women learners encounter are clearly not just internal; significant barriers abound within the institutional environment. As Maher and Tetreault (1994) note, "Until recently, the content and pedagogy of American education, although projecting the 'illusion' that it spoke to everyone, ignored the needs, experiences, and perspectives of the majority of people in this country—women of all backgrounds, people of color, and all women and men who perceive their education as not made for them" (p. 1). Adult women learners, in particular, have faced special challenges as they have reentered (or entered) higher education. Some obvious institutional barriers—such as daytime class schedules, lack of child care, and insensitive school policies (for example, grades dependent on class attendance)—have been addressed with varying success in recent years (Lewis, 1988). But women have had to contend with other barriers besides these. From the time of the medieval university and its successor, the "colonial college"—and despite the admission of the first woman to an American college nearly 150 years ago—institutions of higher education have been designed by and for men (Rudolf, 1977; Belenky, Clinchy, Goldberger, and Tarule, 1986). Small wonder, then, that for most women the classroom can be a "chilly climate" (Hall and Sandler, 1982) that teaches men more effectively than women (Maher and Tetreault, 1994) and constructs knowledge, curricula, and instruction from an androcentric perspective (Minnich, 1990).

However, this climate is slowly changing, due largely to emerging bodies of research and new practices in adult development, adult learning, and feminist pedagogy—three strands of inquiry and experimentation that have converged in alternative, nontraditional degree programs constructed over the past twenty-five years. As educators of adults, we offer a brief perspective on this convergence and provide a historical foundation for many of the educational approaches discussed in this volume.

The alternative higher education programs that sprouted in the 1960s and early 1970s grew out of a desire to reform higher education to be more inclusive of underserved populations (such as "minority," undereducated, incarcerated, and geographically isolated students). Sometime in the mid to late 1970s, educators recognized that this diverse clientele included large numbers of adults and looked to the field of adult education for guidance in serving them. We found relevant historical and philosophical frameworks in Dewey (1938), Freire (1970), Kidd (1973), Knowles (1978), and Lindeman (1926) and added to them the rich experience of alternative education professionals: for example, Cross, Valley, and Associates (1974) and the Carnegie Commission on Higher Education (1971).

Development Theory and Women's Experience

While not exclusively so, alternative higher education has generally been oriented to the individual and particularly to his or her development. By the early 1980s, Chickering and Associates (1981) had proposed, and many adult educators concurred with, development as the aim of education. Practitioners turned again to the growing literature on adult development to help understand life stages and cycles, transitions and transformations, and other kinds of developmental changes that adult learners encounter. Although the research on adult development did help educators respond to the changes that returning students face, it was apparent that the literature focused primarily on men's experience as representative of human experience (see, for example, Erikson, 1959; Levinson, 1978; Perry, 1968). Where women's experiences differed from men's, they were typically labeled deviant or deficient (Caffarella and Olson, 1993). It was clear that these male-based models did not always speak to the experiences of women learners, nor were they wholly applicable to program and curriculum design, teaching, advising, and learning assessment for women students.

Fortunately, practitioners were increasingly able to turn to research in the exciting new arena of feminist pedagogy and, specifically, women's development. This literature named and described women's development in its own terms, offering new theories and new language for how women view themselves (Miller, 1976), how they construct moral questions (Gilligan, 1982), and how social norms and expectations constrain women's development and social roles (Chodorow, 1978; Dinnerstein, 1976). The intuition and experience of educators were captured and validated in these powerful works; we also discovered a remarkable congruence between the practices and philosophies of alternative higher education and these "new" theories and language.

The common threads that emerge from these three bodies of literature (and provide a common theme for this volume) are the validity of students' experience and support for the evolving self as foci of education. The new pedagogy welcomed and explored the contextual nature of knowledge, including the relationship between the student and her knowledge base. The new pedagogy also addressed quite directly the notion of transformative learning (Mezirow, 1991) as well as the multiplicity of ways of knowing and thinking.

Of the many developmental models that effectively illuminate women's experiences, we have selected two to highlight in this sourcebook, because they fit most closely with our experiences as educators of women and as developing women ourselves. We have also found when we teach these models that our women learners feel that these theories most accurately describe their experiences along their journeys of development. Of the two models, *Women's Ways of Knowing* (Belenky, Clinchy, Goldberger, and Tarule, 1986) has more directly influenced educators, helping them understand the strengths and limitations of their approaches and guiding them in reforming their curriculum and teaching practices. Robert Kegan's works, *The Evolving Self* (1982) and the recent *In Over Our Heads* (1994), which authentically include women, underscore the vital importance of directly attending to the learning and developmental needs of adult learners.

Development of Voice. The authors of *Women's Ways of Knowing* (Belenky, Clinchy, Goldberger, and Tarule, 1986) describe five epistemological perspectives: silence, received knowing, subjective knowing, procedural knowing, and constructed knowing. Silence—a disbelief in one's capacity for knowledge—is most often the perspective of severely disenfranchised or abused women. Though our students often identify with having been "silenced" at some point in their lives (and sometimes, still), a truly silent woman is unlikely to be in college: it would not occur to her to claim that place nor that there was any point in doing so.

For received knowers, knowledge resides in others—friends, family members, "authorities" of all kinds; the learner's job is to "get" it from them. These women are likely to look to their teachers for explicit directions, and they are uncomfortable with requests that they be more self-directed. "Whose job is this, anyway?" they are likely to think if asked to take responsibility for their own learning: "I'm the student here—tell me what you want me to do."

A subjective knower has discovered her inner voice and listens to her gut feelings; the source of her knowledge is her intuition. She may experience conflict with the teacher and with texts, since ideas that differ from her intuitive knowledge may be dismissed. "I know what's true for me," a subjective learner is likely to think; she may even express her opinion to her instructors. If she feels threatened by the possibility of disagreement, however, she may go through the motions of reading and reporting the ideas of authorities but will probably not integrate what she is supposedly learning.

Procedural knowers know not only the forms of academic discourse, but also how to dialogue with the text, the author, and the instructor in such a way that their beliefs can be both tested and refined. Two different approaches to creating meaning are found in procedural knowing. As Loughlin and Mott (1992) explain, "in each, a woman has a sense of herself as knower in relation to the known. For a separate knower, her procedures of knowing are objective in relation to the known and are based on logic. . . . [F]or a connected knower, her procedures of knowing involve building a connection to the known and are based on empathy" (p. 81).

In constructed knowing, the final perspective, students have learned to integrate these voices. They have discovered that knowledge comes to them and from them, that their ideas can change or remain the same depending on what they learn from others and what they learn from their own experience and from their reflection on that experience. Constructed knowing integrates experiential and relational modes of thought, reason, and intuition.

The authors of *Women's Ways of Knowing* were divided about whether they should couch these epistemological perspectives as hierarchical, sequential stages or as fluid positions representing qualitatively different strategies—for example, might someone be a procedural knower in one context and a received knower in another? In addition, the authors emphasize that this framework is not, in fact, gender-specific; they refer to it instead as gender-related. Some women do not find their experiences of knowing reflected in this model, whereas many men do. Even so, it has proven to be an effective conceptual tool for understanding how a significant portion of the population approaches knowledge.

Orders of Consciousness. The second major theoretical piece that informs our work with adult women is Kegan's (1982, 1994) model of psychosocial development of both men and women. From an educator's perspective, Kegan's constructive-developmental model is especially profound because it focuses on meaning making: development is a function of perspective transformation. As we develop, we learn to see ourselves and others differently (and to act accordingly) because our lenses of perception change. As they change, we change, because we are, in a fundamental sense, our perceptions. Furthermore, these changes move in the direction of our developing increasingly complex perceptions.

Kegan's model describes five developmental stages or orders of consciousness. At each stage, a person is defined by a particular perspective that determines everything about how she sees the world—her beliefs, communications, perceptions, values, and relationships to others and herself. The first and second orders of consciousness are achieved in infancy and childhood and therefore will not be explored here; nor, given the limited frequency with which it is encountered (1994, p. 195), will the shift from fourth- to fifth-order ("postmodern") consciousness be considered.

The first adult position, third-order consciousness (a blessed relief to parents of adolescents when it happens), is marked by the recognition that others—parents, teachers, social expectations and imperatives (what Kegan calls the psychological surround)—should be featured at least as prominently in the young adult's awareness and decision-making processes as her own needs, wants, and desires. But the shift to a new order of consciousness involves more than just recognition—it is a complete shift to a new way of thinking, a new construction of reality. As a young woman moves into third-order consciousness, the voices of others actually become her own; her relation to the psychological surround is primary and ultimate.

The shift to fourth-order consciousness creates the possibility to choose how, whether, and when an individual will interact with the psychological surround. She can examine it, question it, recognize its flaws, take responsibility for changing it, and even deny its demands. This idea is inconceivable to a woman operating from a third-order consciousness; to question the construction of the surround is to question the construction of the self.

In reentry women, a common signal of the transition from third- to fourth-order consciousness is a change from her feeling guilty, anxious, or uncomfortable about spending time or money or other family resources on her schooling to her recognizing that "it's my turn now" or "things sure have changed at my house." Eventually, perhaps, she will realize that what has changed is her way of thinking about what is happening at her house. And the change to fourth-order consciousness has wide-reaching ramifications because her new perspective of questioning and examining both herself and her immediate surround extends to include her workplace and society at large.

The Role of Education

Education can play a crucial role in this development of consciousness. Unfortunately, many educational environments ask too little—or too much. Those that concentrate on information storage and retrieval—what Freire (1970) calls the "banking" method of education—do not require perspective shifts beyond the third order of consciousness. Instead, the educational environment merges with the psychological surround. However, some innovative educational programs may, with the best of intentions, err in the opposite direction. They may construct learning environments that *require* fourth-order consciousness, rather than provide supports to help it develop. For example, how many learners in programs that emphasize self-direction arrive prepared to fully engage at that level?

We believe that the conceptual frameworks and strategies presented in this sourcebook support development that is consistent with both Belenky and her colleagues' (1986) idea of "self, voice, and mind" and Kegan's (1994) notion of fourth-order consciousness. Many of these approaches were developed before current models of adult and women's development were available. By focusing intuitively on learners' experiences and the construction of the self, educators have been able to create spaces for transformational learning. Mezirow (1991) describes education as a process of learning to transform the meaning we make out of our experience; Kegan (1994) also calls for transformational rather than informational learning in order to meet the "demands of modern life." Learning environments that intentionally support and acknowledge development are bridges toward change, both for reentry students and for the education process itself.

References

Belenky, M. F., Clinchy, B. M., Goldberger, N. R., and Tarule, J. M. *Women's Ways of Knowing: The Development of Self, Voice, and Mind.* New York: Basic Books, 1986.

Caffarella, R., and Olson, S. "Psychological Development of Women: A Critical Review of the Literature." *Adult Education Quarterly,* 1993, 43 (1), 125–151.

Carnegie Commission on Higher Education. *Less Time, More Options—Education Beyond High School.* New York: McGraw-Hill, 1971.

Chickering, A. W., and Associates. *The Modern American College: Responding to the New Realities of Diverse Students and a Changing Society.* San Francisco: Jossey-Bass, 1981.

Chodorow, N. *The Reproduction of Mothering: Psychoanalysis and the Sociology of Gender.* Berkeley: University of California Press, 1978.

"College Enrollment by Age of Students, Fall 1992." *Chronicle of Higher Education Almanac,* Sept. 1, 1994, 41 (1), p. 15.

Cross, K. P., Valley, J. R., and Associates. *Planning Non-Traditional Programs: An Analysis of the Issues for Postsecondary Education.* San Francisco: Jossey-Bass, 1974.

Dewey, J. *Experience and Education.* New York: Collier, 1938.

Dinnerstein, D. *The Mermaid and the Minotaur: Sexual Arrangements and Human Malaise.* New York: HarperCollins, 1976.

Erikson, E. H. *Identity and the Life Cycle.* Psychological Issues Monograph 1. New York: International Universities Press, 1959.

Freire, P. *Pedagogy of the Oppressed.* New York: Continuum, 1970.

Gilligan, C. *In a Different Voice: Psychological Theory and Women's Development.* Cambridge, Mass.: Harvard University Press, 1982.

Hall, R., and Sandler, B. *The Classroom Climate: A Chilly One for Women.* Washington, D.C.: The Project on the Status of Women in Education, 1982.

Kegan, R. *The Evolving Self: Problem and Process in Human Development.* Cambridge, Mass.: Harvard University Press, 1982.

Kegan, R. *In Over Our Heads: The Mental Demands of Modern Life.* Cambridge, Mass.: Harvard University Press, 1994.

Kidd, J. R. *How Adults Learn.* Cambridge, Mass.: Adult Education Company, 1973.

Knowles, M. *The Adult Learner: A Neglected Species.* (2nd ed.) Houston: Gulf, 1978.

Levinson, D. J., Darrow, C., Kline, E., Levinson, M., and McKee, B. *The Seasons of a Man's Life.* New York: Knopf, 1978.

Lewis, L. H. (ed.). *Addressing the Needs of Returning Women.* New Directions for Continuing Education, no. 39. San Francisco: Jossey-Bass, 1988.

Lindeman, E. *The Meaning of Adult Education.* New Republic, 1926.

Loughlin, K., and Mott, V. "Models of Women's Learning: Implications for Continuing Professional Education." In H. K. Morris Baskett and V. J. Marsick (eds.), *Professionals' Ways of Knowing: New Findings on How to Improve Professional Education.* New Directions for Adult and Continuing Education, no. 55. San Francisco: Jossey-Bass, 1992.

Maher, F. A., and Tetreault, M. K. *The Feminist Classroom: An Inside Look at How Professors and Students Are Transforming Higher Education in a Diverse Society.* New York: Basic Books, 1994.

Mezirow, J. *Transformative Dimensions of Adult Learning.* San Francisco: Jossey-Bass, 1991.

Miller, J. B. *Toward a New Psychology of Women.* Boston: Beacon Press, 1976.

Minnich, E. K. *Transforming Knowledge.* Philadelphia: Temple University Press, 1990.

Perry, W. G., Jr. *Forms of Intellectual and Ethical Development in the College Years: A Scheme.* Troy, Mo.: Holt, Rinehart & Winston, 1968.

Rudolf, F. *Curriculum: A History of the American Undergraduate Course of Study Since 1636.* San Francisco: Jossey-Bass, 1977.

KATHLEEN TAYLOR is associate professor at Saint Mary's College of California, chair of the Department of Portfolio Instruction, and a consultant on women's development and education.

CATHERINE MARIENAU is associate professor in the School for New Learning at DePaul University and is active in the Alliance (an association for alternative degree programs for adults).

Women learners discover and construct larger meanings through journal writing.

Journal Writing: A Tool for Women Developing as Knowers

Phyllis Walden

A journal is a powerful teaching and learning tool for helping reentry women develop as knowers. Through guided writing assignments, these women have the opportunity to explore a range of modes of knowing as they examine their lives. They become skilled as knowers, understanding that knowledge is constructed by the self and others and that truth is contextual. I teach a course called The Personal Journal in an adult degree program where enrollments are typically 80 to 90 percent women. Course objectives include teaching effective strategies for keeping a journal and introducing participants to adult development theory. Having taught versions of this course since 1983, I want to highlight teaching and writing strategies that have worked particularly well. While my experience has been primarily with women working on academic degrees, journal writing is also an effective tool, as Gajdusek and Gillotte note in Chapter Six, for women in developmental programs designed to prepare them for college-level work, such as adult basic education and English as a second language programs.

I will describe a variety of writing assignments and techniques that help each woman collect basic information about her life and experience, reflect on the dimensions and evolution of her life, and discover and construct larger meanings. For the woman who has been abused or wounded, a journal is a place where she can begin to talk to herself about the experience and encounter her emerging voice. Through reflective writing, each writer learns to step back from the immediacy of her subjective experience, shift perspective, and generate and examine options. Finally, a journal offers an opportunity to engage in dialogue with the self in ways that further a woman's

New Directions for Adult and Continuing Education, no. 65, Spring 1995 © Jossey-Bass Publishers

development as a constructed knower; it will help her understand the rich context of her life and the questions she faces in her multiple roles.

Preparing to Write

Many women need guidance in getting a journal started—first in discovering that they can, in fact, get words on paper, and second in affirming that they have something to say. I introduce journal writing by focusing on topics and strategies that help to build confidence in a nonthreatening way. I use class time for journal writing and talking about the initial writing experiences. Freewriting and list making are two writing techniques that work particularly well for students starting to use a journal.

Freewriting is writing whatever comes to mind without attention to mechanics, spelling, or grammar (Elbow, 1981). While I suggest a topic as a starting point, I emphasize in the first experiments with freewriting that students are to write whatever comes to mind. The only directions I give are to start writing when I say "start" and to continue writing until I say "stop." A five-minute period focusing on why they are taking the course is a manageable starting point for most students. At the end of five minutes, students read what they have written and write a brief response or reaction. This reflective look at a piece of their own writing, perhaps noting a particular idea, reaction, or response, provides students with a feel for pausing to examine an experience and giving feedback to themselves.

Many students are surprised at both the amount they have written as well as the content. I invite students to share their response to the exercise and/or to read a segment from their writing. Most are excited and eager to write more. A few students find freewriting difficult initially, a situation that can usually be remedied by reassuring them that they *really* do not need to worry about mechanics and spelling. Most participants emphasize throughout the course how valuable freewriting is in learning that writing can be fun and in freeing them to develop their own voices as they create their self-authored identity (see Kegan, 1982). For example, Beth, a student in the course, particularly noted her delight that "it is okay to have three thoughts on the same line."

List making is probably the least threatening writing technique for reentry women, and in some ways, it is the most effective (see Adams, 1990, pp. 123–137). A quick collective "list of lists" that class participants routinely keep will reveal the group's breadth of experience as list makers. I intersperse list making throughout each course as a way of collecting a good deal of information quickly. For example, early in the term I have students make a list of one hundred persons who have influenced them (Adams, 1990). Students initially worry that they cannot possibly make such an extensive list, but they very quickly appreciate how readily list making generates memories and connections, which are often profound and surprising. This list becomes a useful resource in collecting autobiographical material and in developing journal dialogues that engage the writer more deeply. Lists of favorite words, questions, things to write about, and "things I love to do" are assignments most students enjoy. An ongoing list of things to write about provides a place for students to build an agenda for their journals.

In the first class session, a list-making exercise is a useful technique to engage students in collecting information about their current lives. Participants make two lists: a list of endings and a list of beginnings. This is a good time to introduce William Bridges's (1980) theory that transitions in life encompass first an ending, then a neutral zone characterized by uncertainty and confusion, and finally a beginning. Students can use their two lists as a basis both for interpreting excerpts from Bridges's *Transitions* and for looking at their lives from a past, present, and future perspective. The lists of current endings and beginnings quickly captures the multiple components of each woman's "now." Each ending has a history, and each beginning has a future.

Next I have students write a story about one of their endings by starting a freewriting exercise with the phrase, "Once upon a time . . ." Often these stories are written in the third person, which introduces a powerful shift in perspective that is useful for looking at one's life and one's past—a shift from participating in an experience to observing it. Then I have students write a story about a beginning, starting with "In the beginning, . . ." which usually leads the writer into articulating a future possibility as she considers how the beginning might evolve.

List making is a writing strategy students continue to use after the course is over, particularly during times of stress.

> I will find myself making lists. I'll simply start listing what is going on in my life. And I see why things are out of sorts. Then I'll write about one thing on my list for a while. [Kathy]

> I was becoming very frazzled and did not know what was wrong with me. I started listing everything I had to do and where I had to be each evening. When I saw the twenty-plus items on paper, I felt relieved and less disjointed. [Mary Alice]

The simple process of making a list, which is routine for most women, can in fact be an empowering tool for composing oneself and one's life.

Building Observations and Reflections

List making and freewriting about beginnings and endings serve as a starting point. Further assignments help the writer deepen her ability to observe and record her life experience and to identify the significant details that make her life unique. To emphasize the richness of small segments of time, writers identify a period of about one minute to describe in detail. They write about this minute at least twice, a process that usually heightens their awareness of duration and details. Most writers become reflective on the second or third approach. The experience of the moment they write about becomes connected to other moments in their life and to thoughts and ideas that shape their perspective. It is a reminder that individual moments make up the larger framework of beginnings and endings. This exercise helps the writer develop skill in observing and capturing the details of the moments in her life as they occur.

Most students are initially puzzled when this exercise is introduced because they realize they do not know how the span of one minute "feels." However, they quickly see how profound a process it is for examining the layers of meaning embedded in an experience. Linda had noted on her list of things to write about that she wanted to explore a recent visit with her mother. These two entries from her journal show how she develops reflection as she considers a moment from this visit:

> *Entry 1.* I had taken my pictures from the trip out to show my mother and we sit in her living room and we look at the pictures of Kentucky. I was very touched at her interest. I was even more amazed at what I so easily shared with her. I have been on such a different journey than the rest of the family. I found myself sharing my spiritual journey. I told her why I had taken the pictures that I had taken—the series of pictures of the different paths on my walk. My determination to get from the beginning and to come down the road. I was determined not to turn around and retrace my steps. Especially one picture where the large tree lay across the road. I was aware that in the past the tree has stopped me and I have turned around and went back or given up altogether.

> *Entry 2.* What was there about this time that was special? When the question was first asked there was the thought that popped into my mind. I am unsure how to put emotion and feelings into words, let alone written words on a page. I can look back and be aware of the sense of Mother being interested in where I had gone and that she was very pleased that I had some nice memories to enjoy. How long I have longed for her to be interested in me. We talked for a long while. She had always affirmed me in my photography and encouraged me. How do I put down her pride in me? Her caring? She told me the next day how much she enjoyed my visit and the pictures. If I listen, Mother does let her guard down every so often and shows something deep and revealing. It was like I gave her a gift. Was it my journey and the Abbey of Gethsemane? Somehow I think it was more.

While initial one-minute explorations do not always achieve such depth, most students clearly see that they begin in a descriptive mode and become more reflective as they write about their minute a second and third time.

Many strategies can be used for gathering and reflecting on one's life history. Progoff's steppingstones exercise, described in detail in his *At a Journal Workshop* (1975), is particularly rich. Students develop a list of ten to twelve key events or markers in their life. Then, for each period, they freewrite, using the stem, "It was a time when . . ." In exploring each steppingstone period, they examine key events, relationships, changes they recall, and issues they were dealing with in their physical, spiritual, and intellectual lives. This writing is a fruitful source of material for looking at development over time and for identifying patterns and themes that could become organizing principles for further autobiographical writing, as well as for prior learning assessment essays.

I introduce stage theories of adult development while students are completing writing assignments focused on their life history. Students readily connect the ideas of Levinson (1978) and Sheehy (1976) and examine the adequacy of these theories in light of their experiences as women. Often there are examples in the classroom of the theory not reflecting reality, such as when a transition does not happen on schedule or does not happen at all. Students discover that they know something about chronological stage theory from their own experience, that they have the intellectual skills needed to challenge the theory, and that they can participate in the construction of theory by evaluating a particular framework and modifying it to reflect a more inclusive perspective. In the 1990s, for example, students usually challenge race and class limitations of the adult development research that informed Levinson's and Sheehy's work.

Deepening the Context: Constructing Knowledge

Students collect a good deal of information about their current experience and their life history through the writing assignments just described. I next introduce ideas from *Women's Ways of Knowing* (Belenky, Clinchy, Goldberger, and Tarule, 1986) as a framework for deepening understanding of oneself as a knower. In preparation for this discussion, students write about several of the key questions from the book's "voice interview," including, "What relationships have been really important to you and why?" (p. 232) and, "Describe a really powerful learning experience you have had, in or out of school" (p. 234). I then guide them through a journal dialogue, which helps transform the journal from a data bank into a dynamic document that aids in the process of constructing knowledge.

Because students may find the journal dialogue awkward at first, I go through the process with them very slowly and deliberately. First, students consider the list of one hundred people who have touched their lives and review their list of steppingstone life events and their voice interviews. From this they generate a list of persons with whom they feel it would be useful to have a journal conversation. After each student chooses a subject, she writes a focusing statement that summarizes where the relationship is now, what the issues are, and what needs attention. Next, to connect more fully with the subject of the dialogue, they list the other person's steppingstones as fully as possible. For example, a student writing a dialogue with her father would list the major events in his life, in order to approach her writing in the broadest context possible. Participants are then invited to feel the presence of this other person and, as they are ready, greet the individual, let that person respond, and record the dialogue in their journals. Finally, students include a reflective entry about their experience writing the dialogue and their response to reading it.

For many students, this writing exercise is a powerful experience. It often results in a deeper understanding of the complexity of relationships and the difficulty of understanding another person's perspective. Students are frequently visibly emotional as they work on dialogues in class, and they may experience both deep sadness and the joy of feeling connected. Mother-and-child dialogues are common, as are dialogues with parents and spouses. Anna shared a dialogue with the class that captured the complex state of her relationship with her daughter a few days before the daughter's wedding. Another student used the journal dialogue to focus on the inner work required to build a relationship with a child who had developed serious emotional difficulties. By learning to engage in journal dialogues, women learners create spaces for connected conversations, an essential dimension of constructing knowledge.

Journal dialogues need not be restricted to persons. Just as students need to deepen their awareness of themselves as knowers, they also need to broaden their understanding of the overall context of their lives. Therefore I invite students to dialogue in their journals with historical and cultural factors or events that have influenced their lives. These may be personal, such as an accident or illness, or collective, such as the Vietnam War or the Women's movement. An assignment that students find particularly useful for getting an overview of their personal historical context is to read the front page of the *New York Times* from the day of their birth, their tenth birthday, and their twenty-first birthday and to record information and reflections in their journals.

Strauss and Howe's provocative *Generations: A History of America's Future, 1854 to 2069* (1991) has resulted in some spirited conversations—in class and in student journals—about the social and historical contexts in which women's lives emerge. Strauss and Howe argue that there are generational cycles evident in American history; they maintain that approaches to development based on chronological stages, such as Levinson's *Seasons of a Man's Life* (1978) and Sheehy's *Passages* (1976), are, in fact, autobiographies of particular generations.

By working with information about generational cycles, students develop a more complete understanding of the social, political, and cultural dimensions of their lives. Through considering the generational perspective of people who have affected their lives, participants understand more fully how different circumstances have shaped the people who have, in turn, shaped them. Often this results in surprising connections. For example, several students have developed a greater appreciation for family members, particularly grandparents, through considering the generational context and through pursuing dialogue work in their journals. Integrating generational understandings into their journals enables students to construct knowledge by working with basic factual life history information, reflecting on how the broader context has shaped their experiences and those of their significant others, and connecting individual lives to historical developments.

Composing a Life

The journal can be used in three time dimensions: to capture the present, to reflect on one's life history, and to create the future. Assignments that assist women in using the journal to shape the future range from working with daily time management issues to engaging in journal dialogues with oneself at age seventy-five. Students may, for example, develop a list of weekly goals that reflect their multiple responsibilities. They then use their journals and their calendars to plan, and they monitor progress and setbacks in their journals. This is especially helpful early in the term, when students are identifying ways to incorporate journal writing into their lives. A list of "one hundred things I want to do" captures a range of lifetime goals. A year after completing the course, Kathy, who describes her journal as "the land of a thousand lists," notes:

> I thought my one-hundred-item list of things I wanted to do was just a pipe dream. But just writing it down seemed to help me do it. I have in fact done more than twenty-five items on my list, including redoing the front bedroom for my daughter. It is like writing it down makes it more likely that I will do it. I give all of my employees blank journals now and encourage them to make lists and write.

In another writing activity, students imagine themselves five years in the future, and they write the journal entry that they would most like to write on that specific day. A reflective entry focused on identifying goals that are lurking in the first entry helps students connect their future vision of themselves to their daily tasks and actions.

An introduction to basic concepts of women's development theory—coupled with various writing assignments that focus on applying what they have learned—helps women learners to understand their lives more fully and deeply. This enhanced awareness about and continuous construction of their lives is stimulated through ongoing use of their journal. They also learn skills that are applicable in other academic work. They learn that they can write whether they feel like it or not and that they can generate words readily and easily. This enables them to face more formal writing assignments with confidence. Since journal writing is often included in other courses, the opportunity to develop the discipline of writing in a journal regularly and building a repertoire of writing techniques is often valuable in learning more effectively in another course.

References

Adams, K. *Journal to the Self: Twenty-Two Paths to Personal Growth.* New York: Warner Books, 1990.

Belenky, M. F., Clinchy, B. M., Goldberger, N. R., and Tarule, J. M. *Women's Ways of Knowing: The Development of Self, Voice, and Mind.* New York: Basic Books, 1986.

Bridges, W. *Transitions: Making Sense of Life's Changes.* Reading, Mass.: Addison-Wesley, 1980.

Elbow, P. *Writing with Power: Techniques for Mastering the Writing Process.* New York: Oxford University Press, 1981.

Kegan, R. *The Evolving Self: Problem and Process in Human Development.* Cambridge, Mass.: Harvard University Press, 1982.

Levinson, D. J., Darrow, C., Kline, E., Levinson, M., and McKee, B. *The Seasons of a Man's Life.* New York: Knopf, 1978.

Progoff, I. *At a Journal Workshop.* New York: Dialogue House, 1975.

Sheehy, G. *Passages: The Predictable Crises of Adult Life.* New York: Dutton, 1976.

Strauss, W., and Howe, N. *Generations: The History of America's Future, 1854 to 2069.* New York: William Morrow, 1991.

PHYLLIS WALDEN *is dean of continuing education and community services at Morton College in Cicero, Illinois, and a visiting faculty member at the School for New Learning, DePaul University. She writes about and conducts workshops in journal writing.*

Self-assessment leads to greater awareness of one's meaning-making methodology and, hence, more complex meaning.

Sitting Beside Herself: Self-Assessment and Women's Adult Development

Kathleen Taylor

> I now realize that during this course I had trouble writing papers which called for my opinion. But this did not occur when I was trying to write the papers. It only occurred to me right now, as I'm typing this.
>
> —From a student self-assessment

I recently read a mystery story in which the writer provided all the clues for me to figure out "whodunit." I did not figure it out, but thinking about my attempt made it clear to me that I am not always aware of what I know and that I may have to look at what I am aware of in a new way before I can make sense of it, before it means something. Now, a mystery story is a neat puzzle with questions, clues, and answers; but in life, there is a much messier process of knowledge hidden and knowledge revealed—especially when we ourselves are the mystery to be unraveled. Even given Freud's theory of the unconscious, the idea that we need to "discover" something about ourselves seems like a conundrum. After all, how can I *be* who I am and yet not *know* who I am?

But such discoveries tell us something about our own perspective and about why we have not been able to know, or "mean," sooner. They also reveal how we make sense of the "clues," and in this way, we begin to understand the rules by which we construct or make meaning. If we pay close attention, we may even realize that these rules become ever more complex as we go through life. This increasingly sophisticated construction of meaning is, in fact, what is

New Directions for Adult and Continuing Education, no. 65, Spring 1995 © Jossey-Bass Publishers

called "development." Unfortunately, we are rarely invited to pay this kind of attention to our meaning making in most classrooms.

Because this sourcebook is about relationships between learning and development, I will explore how cultivating an awareness of one's meaning-making methodology helps one make more complex meaning. I will look specifically at the role of self-assessment in this process, although structured journals and prior experiential learning essays, when highly self-reflective and self-analytical, may produce similar results (see Chapters Two and Four).

According to Kegan's constructive-developmental model (1982, 1994), each stage of development is a function of, and is defined by, a particular perceptual framework (that is, a rule for making meaning). A person's perceptual framework is like a pair of glasses she does not know she is wearing. These lenses affect what is perceived, but since the person does not know they are there, what she perceives (so far as she is able to discern it) is "reality." Development occurs when the "prescription" of the lenses changes and the person perceives a larger, more complex reality. How does a person's prescription change? By her recognizing it for what it is—perception. But how does that happen? How does one have a reality and see it too?

Looking *at* one's perceptual framework while also looking *through* presents the same kind of paradox as pulling oneself up by one's bootstraps; both activities require one to be in two places at the same time. To pull myself up by my own bootstraps, I must be both where I wish to be (the position from which I will be doing the pulling) and also where I presently am (where my boots, and therefore my bootstraps, are). Similarly, in order for me to recognize that my reality is just that—my construction—I must be both inside my reality and outside it.

Educators typically associate assessment with tests and grades. The word *assess*, however, is from the Latin for "to sit beside." Self-assessment, therefore, can be seen as sitting beside the self (the ideal—indeed the only—position from which it is possible to bootstrap). From this position, I can observe myself observing, perceive myself perceiving, and examine myself creating the reality that creates who I am. I can therefore examine my belief in the reality I perceive, with the knowledge that this reality is the creation of my perceptions; this dialogue will, in turn, change those perceptions and that reality—and therefore me.

In the context of most educational programs, self-assessment is both a process and a product: it is an act of self-reflection as well as a written exercise that may be assigned at various points as a learner's education progresses to help her focus on her process of learning (Taylor and Marienau, 1993). Self-assessments may be either open-ended or structured (Waluconis, 1993); the essential element is to ask questions that invite the learner to examine how she learns. (See MacGregor, 1993; she describes various prompts in the appendix to her sourcebook on student self-evaluation.) In so doing, the learner makes discoveries both about the subject matter and about herself. Initially she will make discoveries about herself as a learner; later her self-discovery may become more global.

Developing Voices

In a self-assessment written at the end of her first course after reentry, a woman in her mid forties describes her new self-awareness.

> I have learned how to watch how I think, what happens when I think different ways, and how to be more flexible in the thinking process. I now have more choices about what and how to think. I have begun to find a voice. An interesting thing along the way is that, once I was able to voice my thoughts, what I thought about something often changed and moved to a higher level.

Her awareness of her construction of self-as-knower has led to a greater awareness of her construction of self. In addition, the significance of her finding her voice echoes the conclusion of Belenky, Clinchy, Goldberger, and Tarule (1986) that women's ways of knowing embody the development of self, voice, and mind.

The development of self—of identity—is a recurrent theme for reentry women. Following are two women's descriptions of the experiences that surrounded their return to school. The first is from a single, highly successful professional woman in her mid thirties:

> I didn't know where I was, who I was or—it's as if I was somebody and was trying to be somebody *else*, but didn't know who that other person was going to be at the end of the tunnel; and in between all of that, I wasn't anyone myself.

The second is from a mother of two in her late thirties, married to a career military man for seventeen years:

> I didn't know who I was, what I wanted, where I wanted to be . . . I almost couldn't even go in and take a shower in the morning without forgetting what I was supposed to do next.

To return to an earlier metaphor, the prescriptions of these women's lenses of perception were being changed, but the new glasses were not ready yet. The literature of adult development describes these experiences as *transitions;* they are comparable to what Bridges (1980) calls the "neutral zone" (phase two of his multipart transition process), and they are often experienced as a state of breakdown, chaos, or limbo. However, depending on a woman's overall feelings about change, on where she is in the process, and on her external supports—or lack thereof—transitions can also be energizing and exhilarating. For example, as Heather wrote in her self-assessment for her first course in a degree-completion program:

> At this point in the roller-coaster ride [of this course], I am at a peak where I can look down on what is waiting for me [to finish the degree] and feel the

excitement mount. All the support structures seem to be in place for a secure ride, although a wild one.

Developmentally speaking, a woman in transition is neither who she was nor who she will be; she is still *someone,* of course, but she is often not at all sure just who that is. One way out of this quandary is to name and explore her confusion, for in her examination of who she is not, who she is emerges.

Tracking Development

Using the developmental frameworks developed by Kegan (1982, 1994) and Belenky, Clinchy, Goldberger, and Tarule (1986), I will trace Burdette's progress in a degree-completion program through excerpts from three of her self-assessments:

> *End of first quarter.* I have discovered it is all right to feel awkward, confused, scared, ignorant, unintelligent, and the list goes on and on. The trick is to close your eyes, open your mind and dig into the learning process.

> *Several months later.* I felt overwhelmed . . . with putting my thoughts on paper. . . . I do not have difficulty expressing my opinions verbally, but do have difficulty with stating my opinions in a way that seems more open to scrutiny. . . . This learning made me very aware of how frequently my thinking was criticized as I was growing up.

> *A few weeks before graduation.* I started [this program] with an extremely low self-confidence and practically no self-esteem. I know that somewhere I had those things, but had no idea how to tap into that knowledge. . . . [Now] I have found that I have choices, more than one. I have a life that is separate from anyone else and . . . I need not worry that I am wrong when I cannot control my life. . . . I have given up the control of others and am willing to let them be themselves.

The first excerpt provides a revealing baseline of both bravery and vulnerability in Burdette. Her subsequent reluctance to express her opinions in ways that are "open to scrutiny" suggests the theory presented in *Women's Ways of Knowing* (Belenky, Clinchy, Goldberger, and Tarule, 1986). Being able to express herself—to have a voice, speak out, speak for herself, voice her opinion—is part of her being able to know at all, in addition to her being able to know who she is. In order for women to develop their minds and identities, they must also develop their voice—they must become comfortable with their voice and be willing to express it. In this regard, self-assessment can be likened to singing in the epistemological shower.

Burdette's description of her finding her voice suggests a move from received to subjective knowing; her later perception of increased flexibility of thought and an ability to examine her own assumptions and choices suggests that she is developing beyond subjectivism toward procedural knowing (see Chapters One and Seven and Belenky, Clinchy, Goldberger, and Tarule, 1986).

Her final self-assessment also echoes the meaning structures in Kegan's model (1982, 1994), which suggests that most adults in this society are negotiating a transition between an identity defined by the psychological surround (see Chapters One and Ten) and one that is self-authored. This woman has not only discovered "a life that is separate from anyone else"; she has also discovered that she no longer needs to control those around her—and that she is less likely to be controlled by them. Though she might not yet fully realize it, allowing others to be themselves is the other half of the equation that allows her to be herself. She also recognizes choices that were invisible to her before. To have choices means that the absolutes and imperatives of third-order consciousness—the result of internalizing the voices and values of the psychological surround—have given way to self-regulation and self-authorization, which is the wellspring of identity and individuation.

Of course, self-assessment is not the only factor contributing to this growth; but the requirements of development—that we become aware of our rules of meaning making, so that we can see that we have made the meaning which governs our lives—suggest that such self-reflection is certainly an important part.

Mirroring Growth

As it reflects growing awareness, self-assessment encourages aspects of self, such as self-responsibility and self-direction, to emerge more powerfully. This emergence is developmental growth.

Enhancing Self-Responsibility. Even reflections that do not seem at first to be developmentally significant may in fact be so. For example, in describing her challenges and accomplishments during a course of study, a woman can come to acknowledge her own contribution to both her successes and her failures. This is an important step beyond seeing herself as someone to whom things happen or someone who must respond to a situation. Rather, she is someone who exercises her skills and makes choices. Specifically, reentry women often shrug off good grades, seeing them as the result of luck or a kindly or easy instructor. Similarly, if they are unable to complete an assignment due to external demands, they may fail to see their own role in permitting the interruption. Self-assessment can begin to reveal the flaws in these constructions of reality. One woman, at the end of a course for which she had to request an incomplete, made this observation:

> Cleaning and reorganizing my new residence . . . suddenly became life-threatening. I told myself over and over again that I would unpack just one box or straighten out just one room. Days later I would still be unpacking and straightening. I now realize I used these things as a means of rationalizing the fact that my paper was not going to be completed on time.

Given the tardy submission of her paper, her realization may seem a small victory; indeed, she still distances herself from full responsibility by using passive voice in the last sentence. Nevertheless, she has caught herself in the act—a realization that requires being in two positions at the same time: one, the developmental position she is leaving behind; the other, the position she is growing toward.

Enhancing Self-Direction. Another contribution self-assessment makes to development is to enhance women's awareness of themselves as central to the learning process. Although as a rule reentry women return to school highly motivated to do well and to learn (and they are often acknowledged as the best students on campus), their perception of how to learn is often focused on doing "what the teacher wants." Self-assessment can help such women rethink the relationship between teaching and learning and thereby recognize and enhance their capacity for self-direction, which, Kegan (1994) tells us, indicates a movement toward fourth-order consciousness.

Enhancing Perceptual Shift. In general, self-assessment appears to have outcomes similar to the open-ended interviews conducted by Perry (1968) and by Belenky, Clinchy, Goldberger, and Tarule (1986). For example, when students heard themselves reflect on salient, if confusing, learning experiences, their perceptions changed *as* they reflected. Perry found that their "reports of such moments . . . reveal, both implicitly and explicitly, (a) the structure of the earlier experiences which had proved inadequate, (b) the structure of the new interpretation which resolved the incongruity, and (c) the transitional process by which the new structure was created" (p. 42).

In a similar vein, one student described the importance of communicating to herself—particularly when self-assessment, which she described as "valuable but painful," brought her face-to-face with unresolved issues:

> I always hated those self-assessments . . . because I really didn't know how to deal with whatever the issue was . . . so the self-assessment was, like, "Oh, god, I have to deal with this." . . . [Because] when you actually write it, *especially to yourself,* it gives it more power. It's one thing to write about racists and racism [in term papers] and how it affects the African American, but another thing to write about racism and how it affects me [emphasis added].

Enhancing Self-Questioning. When reentry women examine the perceptual framework they use in defining themselves as learners, they tend also to question their *overall* meaning-making perspectives, opening up possibilities for new ones to be created. Self-assessment becomes a generalizable skill that enables them to examine other aspects of their lives, sometimes leading to dramatic change. "Why didn't you tell me self-assessment wouldn't stop at the schoolhouse door?" asked one woman, who separated from her partner shortly afterward.

Students Not Ready to Self-Assess

Student self-assessments are not always a doorway to developmental progress; not everyone is developmentally ready to "sit beside the self," or they may not know how—they may not know what a self-assessment looks like or how valuable it is. We need to provide guidance, initially perhaps in the form of questions for reflection and certainly in the form of positive feedback whenever self-assessment accomplishes the desired end of truly self-reflective observation. (For specific instructions on how to teach and use self-assessments, consult the excellent sourcebook edited by MacGregor, 1993).

Some "self-assessments" never, in fact, focus on the self: they describe the teacher, the content of the course, even the layout of the room—anything but the self. Others contain words of self-discovery that sound hollow or formulaic, as if the learner has repeated a phrase in a language she does not truly understand. At other times, a learner's self-assessments sound repetitious. This may be analogous to the holding pattern Perry (1968) identified as *temporizing*—a sort of developmental breather while the person prepares for the next uphill climb.

Conclusion

Finally, we return to the significance of self-assessment in developing a woman's sense of self—in helping her discover who she is. As she reflects on what she has learned, on her process of learning, on her perceived successes and failures, and on her awareness of her perceptions—expressing new and still forming ideas—self-assessment may provide "the first tentative affirmations of a position the student knows to be on her leading edge, ideas too risky to entertain outside the safety of this space, a still tender voice speaking itself into being" (Daloz, 1986, pp. 221–222). As their voices grow stronger and clearer, the speakers do also.

> I am much less inhibited and guarded by virtue of the fact that self-assessment has revealed a me that I like and accept.

> As a result of doing self-assessment, I no longer view making mistakes as a character flaw.

> Self-assessment is gradually giving me the sense that success doesn't mean doing everything perfectly all the time; but rather that one can grow and improve through setbacks.

> My increasing ability to engage in self-assessment has become the strong foundation upon which all other learning has been built.

References

Belenky, M. F., Clinchy, B. M., Goldberger, N. R., and Tarule, J. M. *Women's Ways of Knowing: The Development of Self, Voice, and Mind.* New York: Basic Books, 1986.

Bridges, W. *Transitions: Making Sense of Life's Changes.* Reading, Mass.: Addison-Wesley, 1980.

Daloz, L. A. *Effective Teaching and Mentoring: Realizing the Transformational Power of Adult Learning Experiences.* San Francisco: Jossey-Bass, 1986.

Kegan, R. *The Evolving Self: Problem and Process in Human Development.* Cambridge, Mass.: Harvard University Press, 1982.

Kegan, R. *In Over Our Heads: The Mental Demands of Modern Life.* Cambridge, Mass.: Harvard University Press, 1994.

MacGregor, J. (ed.). *Student Self-Evaluation: Fostering Reflective Learning.* New Directions for Teaching and Learning, no. 56. San Francisco: Jossey-Bass, 1993.

Perry, W. G., Jr. *Forms of Intellectual and Ethical Development in the College Years: A Scheme.* Troy, Mo.: Holt, Rinehart & Winston, 1968.

Taylor, K., and Marienau, C. "Self-Assessment, Discovery of Self, and Self-Development in the Adult Learner." *Contemporary Education,* 1993, *64* (3), 166–169.

Waluconis, C. J. "Self-Evaluation: Settings and Uses." In J. MacGregor (ed.), *Student Self-Evaluation: Fostering Reflective Learning.* New Directions for Teaching and Learning, no. 56. San Francisco: Jossey-Bass, 1993.

KATHLEEN TAYLOR is associate professor at Saint Mary's College of California, chair of the Department of Portfolio Instruction, and a consultant on women's development and education.

When it teaches critical self-reflection, prior learning assessment
encourages developmental growth in adult women.

Prior Learning Assessment, Critical Self-Reflection,, and Reentry Women's Development

Jan Droegkamp, Kathleen Taylor

> Something inside me clicked when I told my college advisor that I
> wanted to explore getting some college credits for my life experi-
> ences. A tiny voice said, "Jenny, you *are* someone and you have
> done wonderful and important things." This was a new discovery—
> I was ready to begin my new journey.
>
> —A reentry woman

One of the enduring innovations of alternative higher education is the recognition and assessment of learning from life experience. In this chapter, we will
use the term *prior learning assessment* (PLA) to describe a variety of approaches
that allow students to receive undergraduate credits for extramural learning.
We do not intend to advocate the use of PLA for credit per se nor to compare
how various programs construct their PLA component, but focus instead on
aspects of PLA that can promote adult development.

Many women return to college with long lists of personal and professional skills and knowledge acquired outside of formal academic settings. The
Council on Adult and Experiential Learning (CAEL), a nationally recognized
pioneer in establishing standards and methods for gaining academic credit for
prior learning, has described elements of an academically sound approach
to PLA (Whitaker, 1989). Probably the most widespread practices are to
award credit based on (1) scores on standardized exams; (2) course work
completed in noncollegiate environments such as the military, corporations,

and government agencies; (3) professional licenses, certificates, or apprenticeships; and (4) successful "challenging" of courses by students, usually by passing final exams.

PLA Approaches That Support Development

The most developmentally effective approach to PLA, however, focuses on self-reflective essays in which students critically examine their experiences in terms of college-level learning outcomes. Other developmentally significant components of PLA include a statement that provides a context for the learner's goals, often as part of or in addition to an autobiography, and a chronological record of significant learning experiences.

A *goals statement* allows women to acknowledge where they have been and what they have accomplished and to imagine a different future. Creating goals statements often involves clarifying students' roles, identity, and perspective—stepping "out of the systems that have governed their lives" (Belenky, Clinchy, Goldberger, and Tarule, 1986, p. 128). As one student noted, writing the goals section of the portfolio

> helped me see my life options. I felt empowered—I could dream my vision of the future and actually accomplish my long-term goals. Just writing those thoughts down gave me such energy and motivation.

Similarly, the *chronological record,* an inventory of all significant adult learning experiences, can combine with an *autobiography* to help a woman form a holistic picture of her life. Women often gain insight into their current life and choices through an analysis of their past relationships with family, friends, co-workers, teachers, and mentors. They may also identify new or different patterns which reveal to them something about their own constructions of reality. According to Kegan (1982), this recognition—that we construct reality as we interpret our experiences—is a cornerstone of development. As one woman, a thirty-nine-year-old professional, observed:

> Writing my portfolio was a life-changing process. I felt I was able to do what I wanted to do, versus what I had to do. Writing my autobiography helped me define where I was going, what I had done, and where my life could take me. I saw my life as a process; the journey was hard. The most important part for me was that I discovered I had a voice and used it for the first time in writing about who I was.

Writing an autobiography often helps a woman find her voice. As Belenky, Clinchy, Goldberger, and Tarule (1986) point out, it can be an important step in the developmental journey of establishing identity and recognizing the power of her own mind.

Experiential Learning Essays and Self-Discovery

In writing a *narrative* or *experiential learning essay,* the student must analyze her own experiences and relate them to theories and principles—her own and others'—to help describe her learning in a manner appropriate to an academic context. The process of writing the essay is developmentally significant on two counts.

First, experiential learning essays mirror growth (Taylor, 1994). They enable the reentry woman to acknowledge how far she has come (and sometimes, against what odds). Even women with noteworthy professional achievements discover that writing an experiential learning essay provides, as one student put it, "a real sense of accomplishment. . . . You find out you know a lot more than you thought you did."

For women who have not had impressive careers, being able to document their experiential learning may be even more significant. Such women may, as Knowles says, "have little to sustain their dignity other than their experience" (1984, p. 11). For example, a woman who had been brought up to think of herself as stupid described her reaction to writing PLA essays.

> We [wrote about] previous learning . . . [what I already] knew at that point. So I felt kind of positive. Once I got those things [written] I felt good, and that brought on personal changes. . . . It made me have to look within myself for answers . . . and it led to more and more. That was definitely the beginning of a big growth . . . because I was being, in a weird way, kind of reassured that I knew something.

Another woman described how the extremely challenging process of writing an experiential learning essay led her to a new appreciation of herself.

> I am a new person. When I came here I felt worthless, uncomfortable in a college setting with people who knew so much more than I. . . . [Now I] appreciate what I have to offer—that I am someone who knows something. I am a better listener, a better parent, and I trust myself now.

These women's descriptions validate Belenky, Clinchy, Goldberger, and Tarule's observation (1986) that women in their study did not "wish to be told merely that they had the capacity or the potential to become knowledgeable or wise. They needed to know that they already knew something." PLA, then, can be a mirror wherein women can catch the reflection of "something good inside them" (p. 195).

Second, PLA essays demand a level of critical self-reflection and of questioning one's assumptions (one's reality) that is, within the framework of Kegan's model (1982, 1994), diagnostic for development. Not all students are initially capable of this kind of substantive reflection or analysis. Received and subjective knowers (see Chapters One and Seven and Belenky, Clinchy, Gold-berger, and Tarule, 1986) and women at Kegan's third order of consciousness (1994) may have difficulty understanding the purpose and method of the crit-ically self-reflective essay. "Will you tell me what it is I know?" asked one woman. Other students may find it difficult to write analytically about experi-ences that are still too recent or emotionally unresolved, such as a painful divorce or the death of someone dear. But the process of putting their thoughts and feelings on paper is often a necessary first step toward developing the dis-tance and (relative) objectivity that may eventually make self-analysis possible.

As we tell our students when they attempt to write PLA essays, there is no college course in "Sonja's divorce," but there is one in the sociology of divorce. For college credit, Sonja will have to learn to frame and explore her particular experiences using the language and concepts general to an appropriate disci-pline (in this instance, sociology); she must learn to look *at* her experience rather than *through* it. When people engaging in self-reflective narratives begin to understand how and why they have made the choices they have made, they enter into a new relationship with their experience—and with themselves. One woman's end-of-course reflection on writing experiential learning essays echoes this change.

> As I went back and reread my essays, one last time, and one last time, and one last time, it seemed to me . . . [I wrote about] the way I choose to live, rather than how I think I should live.

Kegan (1994) calls this new relationship with themselves fourth-order consciousness. Its hallmark is the capacity to observe and question former imperatives, constructions, and truths; it is also the destination that most adults in this society are journeying toward. Those who are still at the third order of consciousness cannot question what is, for them, reality—the voices, beliefs, values, imperatives, and constructions of the psychological surround. (For further discussion of the orders of consciousness and Kegan's model, see Chapters One and Ten.)

Reaching toward a new level of consciousness can be a harrowing—as well as exhilarating—experience, however. This journey of consciousness requires a bridge between where the learner is and where she is going. Kierkegaard's observation, quoted by Kegan (1994), that "instruction begins when you put yourself in [the student's] place so that you may understand what [she] understands and in the way [she] understands it" (p. 278) tells edu-cators how to create one set of pillars for that bridge. But the requirements of the self-analytical PLA essay—to examine one's experience through the lens of, for example, a disciplinary framework—can help *the learner* begin to identify what she understands and to examine the way in which she understands it. This is echoed by a woman who found that PLA helped her better understand her life.

It was very important for me to [know where I came from and to] put that together. It looked to me like I'd been this fragmented person . . . [but] I was able to see how much work I had done in my life and that [it] didn't fit the usual pattern. . . . It was a bridge for me. I really don't think that without [PLA] I'd have gotten the clarity I have. [I was able to] go back and make sense out of what has happened in the past.

Carolyn Heilbrun (1988) suggests that women must write their lives in order to reclaim their power. There is a relationship, she says, between a woman's selfhood and her own story. "Women have been deprived of the narratives . . . by which they might assume power over—take control of—their own lives" (p. 17). For example, one woman in a PLA program was accustomed to responding to everyone else's needs; she was the quintessential volunteer—president of the board of a battered woman's shelter, member of the board of a hospital auxiliary and a children's center, tireless worker on local and state political campaigns, organizer of bake sales and school trips, producer of a newsletter for her church. But she felt that she was "perceived as a worker and not a thinker." As she wrote her goals statement, she was able to voice her own desires:

In the next couple of years I want to take some art classes just for me. I have wanted to do that since I was a small child, but my parents, and now my husband, said that . . . time devoted to that [would be] wasteful.

For women like this, the self-reflective, personal-narrative aspects of the PLA process are an opportunity and a challenge to regain—or develop—a sense of self.

Though most students initially regard PLA as a way to save time and money, they soon find that writing experiential learning essays can be considerably more taxing than taking a class. But many students become so enthralled with a sense of self-discovery that their initial reason for pursuing PLA—accumulating college credits—becomes secondary. One woman did not even submit her completed portfolio for credit assessment; she said it was the process that had been of real value to her. She had initially expressed reservations: "I didn't know what I would write about. My life has been boring and all messed up." Four months later, she recognized that her life was worth attention—and that she had choices.

Teaching PLA Skills

PLA skills may be taught in an initial course, seminar, or workshop, or they may be addressed as an ongoing part of a student's reentry program. This learning experience has benefits beyond academic credits or development. Many women reenter the academic world after long absences. Their levels of academic self-esteem vary widely. While they may be sure of themselves at home or work, they may be unsure of their academic skills and abilities. A process that focuses on past learning and achievement helps women feel that they are starting with a sound foundation in the skills required in the classroom; the process welcomes women with various abilities and helps them find their own voice, providing a positive entry into an unfamiliar world. Moreover, this type of learning-centered pedagogy may support the developmental process (see Chapter Nine). In many institutions, the PLA process provides an opportunity for these benefits.

PLA courses may include information on learning styles and on learning how to learn, providing a framework for students to analyze their experiences. Such courses also encourage development of academic skills, including oral and written communication, reflective and critical thinking, and analysis and evaluation. And because of their emphasis on experience as learning, such courses can be particularly helpful to students who have been away from academic settings for an extended time.

In addition to explaining PLA principles and offering assistance in documenting experiential learning for assessment, some PLA processes have recently begun to introduce students to theories of adult learning and adult development. This follows from the growing realization that, for most reentry students, returning to school signals an impending transformation, and PLA may accelerate that process. Information about adult growth and development helps prepare learners for the kind of change they are likely to experience. (For further exploration of the impact of teaching adult development theory, see Chapter Five.)

Two Caveats

Not everyone experiences developmental growth during the PLA process. Some students write serviceable, creditable essays that do not appear to lead to significantly increased self-knowledge. Given the widespread practice of documenting experience in course-equivalent chunks, this may be an indictment of a process that on the one hand acknowledges the value of experience, but that on the other hand "may or may not be appropriate to the learning as it was experienced" (Kytle and Zencey, 1994, p. 7). Other learners may be overwhelmed by the possibility, even if it is only unconsciously perceived, of moving from their current position of comfort. As Kegan notes, "any move which disrupts our supports—and especially to a place where such supports are not likely to be easily replaceable—is bound to be painful" (1982, p. 192).

We would also like to acknowledge a new controversy brewing in the PLA community. Kytle and Zencey (1994) ask whether the concept of assessing *prior* learning is appropriate, since there is good evidence that the bulk of what educators define as learning occurs during the process of preparing for assessment. They also ask whether the common approach of asking students to present their experiences in the form of course equivalents does not in important ways invalidate the breadth, nuances, and generalizability of that experience. (Life rarely teaches according to a syllabus.) There may really be two issues here—the semantics of designating this potentially rich process as "prior" learning and the general, though not universal, practice of assessing learning through the lens of academic disciplines. Disciplines, after all, are simply organizers of ideas; however, disciplinarity often leads to a view of learning that denies the rich interrelatedness of knowledge and its uses. When real interdisciplinary learning arrives at the academic doorstep, the tendency is to honor it only when it fits into established disciplinary molds.

Conclusion

As Malcolm Knowles (1984) observed, to not value a person's experiences is to not value the person. Validating—and more importantly, awarding academic credit for—a woman's experiential learning affirms the significance of her "real-life" accomplishments (Taylor, 1994) and thus bolsters her self-esteem and self-confidence. She also increases her academic self-esteem as she builds a foundation of knowledge upon which she can draw during her reentry program. Most significantly, processes that require a student to examine and explore her life, to articulate her goals and dreams, to describe the significance to her understanding (of herself or the world at large) of her experiences and observations—these are the processes that encourage discovery and development of her self, voice, and mind, of an identity that is self-authored and self-defined.

After turning in her portfolio of experiential learning essays, a thirty-four-year-old single mother wrote:

> It was tremendously exciting to finally grasp the concept—kind of like Helen Keller and W-A-T-E-R. . . . [What] will stay with me . . . will [be] the constant habit of trying to draw conclusions from multiple experiences. . . . I can see in my daily work the changes through looking at things differently, more globally, more critically. After [this experience] I feel I can handle anything.

References

Belenky, M. F., Clinchy, B. M., Goldberger, N. R., and Tarule, J. M. *Women's Ways of Knowing: The Development of Self, Voice, and Mind.* New York: Basic Books, 1986.

Heilbrun, C. G. *Writing a Woman's Life.* New York: Ballantine Books, 1988.

Kegan, R. *The Evolving Self: Problem and Process in Human Development.* Cambridge, Mass.: Harvard University Press, 1982.

Kegan, R. *In Over Our Heads: The Mental Demands of Modern Life.* Cambridge, Mass.: Harvard University Press, 1994.

Knowles, M. S., and Associates. *Andragogy in Action: Applying Modern Principles of Adult Learning.* San Francisco: Jossey-Bass, 1984.

Kytle, J., and Zencey, E. "Of Carts, Horses, and Trojan Gifts: The Transformative Task of Prior Learning Assessment." *CAEL Forum and News,* Summer 1994, pp. 7–10.

Taylor, K. "Teaching to Support Women's Adult Development." *Thought & Action,* 1994, *10* (1), 57–72.

Whitaker, U. *Assessing Learning: Standards, Principles, and Procedures.* Philadelphia: Council on Adult and Experiential Learning, 1989.

JAN DROEGKAMP *is professor of experiential learning at Sangamon State University and directs the Credit for Prior Learning program. She teaches nontraditional education, women's studies, and international studies courses.*

KATHLEEN TAYLOR *is associate professor at Saint Mary's College of California, chair of the Department of Portfolio Instruction, and a consultant on women's development and education.*

*Linking women's experiences with theories of women's development as
course content contributes to women's development.*

In Their Own Voices: Women Learning
About Their Own Development

Catherine Marienau

> I came here ready to fight for space, fight for a voice, and I find I am learning
> with the knowledge that was mine all along—inside me—waiting to be set free.
> Thanks for helping to create a place for that to happen.

This is Jane's journal entry, written near the end of an undergraduate course,
Women's Psychosocial Development, that I teach in an adult degree program.
Jane is forty-four, a divorced mother of three, and an excommunicated member of a fundamentalist Christian sect. She has been estranged from her now-
fourteen-year-old daughter for four years, ever since she answered yes to her
daughter's query about whether she was a lesbian. Jane grew up in a house-
hold she describes as a madhouse. "It felt like our lives [hers and her sister's]
were reviewed and judged on a daily basis," she says. "We knew death waited
just behind that one rageful incident my father could not control." One won-
ders not that Jane came to the course "ready to fight," but that she had any
fight left in her.

Meeting the Woman Within

To look at the other women sitting in a semicircle the first night of class, presenting their public faces, one would have little inkling that their lives are, for
the most part, as dramatic and complex as Jane's. In the ten years I have been

I wish to acknowledge the women learners at the School for New Learning, DePaul
University, whose self-reports I have drawn on, and to thank my colleague Morris Fiddler
for helping me reflect on what I have learned from them.

teaching this course, I have come to understand that the extraordinary experiences of Jane's life are different only in degree from the complex realities of the lives of most reentry women. Such experiences among the students are found in every course I teach. Students in a typical class of mine range in age from the mid twenties to early sixties, cut across racial and ethnic lines (a typical class is 65 percent Caucasian, 20 percent African American, and 15 percent Latina), and bring wide-ranging experiences from work and family histories.

"As far back as I can remember, I don't recall feeling good about myself," writes a Latina woman in her forties in the first sentence of her self-description. Many women echo this feeling. Many also raise the question, "Who am I?" A woman in her fifties asks, "When do you come to know that you cannot define yourself by how others see you?" The crippling effects of alcohol and drug abuse are another recurring theme, and a surprising incidence of physical and psychological abuse is revealed. One woman reports that "I feel I was a lost child, having been raised by an alcoholic father, whose needs surpassed the needs of a little child." Another woman writes of the "shame that came from my father's alcoholism and trying to live out the myth of a normal home." An African American woman in her thirties speaks, with tears quietly flowing, about how hard it is to break away from the constraining, sometimes abusive, embrace of her mother. And many women describe a major significant loss through the death of a spouse or child or through divorce or other dramatic separation from their family.

Regardless of each woman's history, returning to school often brings out feelings of inadequacy—for some, a feeling close to terror—about meeting the challenges of academic life: "School is extremely intimidating for me—everyone is smarter than I am"; "I have such anxiety about returning to school—I am sure I cannot make it"; or, "I have such huge gaps in my knowledge, how can I ever begin to fill them in?"

None of this is immediately evident as we make introductions and begin to engage in conversation with each other. But over the course of the next ten weeks, some of the many challenges these women face are made more visible to themselves and to me. As they write journal assignments and enter into a dialogue with the material, we come to see that the various themes of development and change described in the readings are also manifest in their lives. They have experienced a sense of losing themselves in relationships (Kegan, 1982), of feeling inadequate in their knowing and ways of knowing (Belenky, Clinchy, Goldberger and Tarule, 1986). There are also themes of reaching for more, of overcoming and persevering, and of caring for and about oneself.

Developing Through Learning

How does learning about development support these women in their own process of development? I have found that exposure to models and theories of adult women's development offers women learners structures and language that they can use to make sense of the varied and complex experiences they bring with them to class. They can begin to conceptualize—to think about and interpret—their experiences, not just undergo them.

As a result, they begin to examine their life history from a new perspective. Such transformations in perspective are, according to Mezirow (1991), at the heart of development. They also begin to observe their engagement in current experiences—as those experiences unfold. This capacity to step back and critically examine one's own emotional and thought processes is also a hallmark of development (Kegan, 1982).

For several years, I have asked learners completing my course to respond in writing to a version of this question: "How has learning about women's development contributed to your understanding of self and to your own development?" I have limited the in-depth analysis of the responses presented here to responses from the last three course offerings, held in 1993, 1990, and 1989, because these courses were the most similar in the material presented. I identified six recurrent themes in the responses of approximately sixty-five women learners: knowing oneself, accepting oneself, connecting with others, changing perspectives, empowering oneself, and seeking growth and development. The following are the rich and varied voices of women learners describing the impact that learning about their development has had on their sense of self.

Knowing Oneself

Learning about women's development has actually put some of the pieces back together for me. It has allowed me to explore and search for aspects of my life and of my self that have been difficult. . . . It has given me . . . validation of my existence in the life I lead.

This course has given me the language that I need to begin to find a voice in articulating what my experience has been and what it means.

I have discovered that it is possible to function as an adult, to play out the roles assigned to us, and to keep busy and to react in certain situations without spending a lot of time examining [my]self. I have discovered that it is possible to function in a mode where self-esteem is not examined.

Accepting Oneself

The negative self-image I once had about myself is slowly, and a little late, going away. It has produced a change from a negative self-image to clearly a more positive self-image.

Reading the works of women who devote their time to the understanding of women's ways of knowing not only increased my knowledge but it helped build my self-confidence.

I have begun to understand how many different factors contribute to a woman's sense of self and self-esteem. When you begin to think about yourself in a different context, you discover strengths you never knew you had.

Connecting with Others

I think I have always gotten a lot out of my friendships [and] relationships, and now I feel more secure in them in that they are contributing to my development—and this is good. . . . This class especially has helped me realize important things about my relationships with family, friends, and my husband.

Learning about women's development has validated some things for me—that it's OK to be relationship-oriented, that it's OK to be a caretaker, or not to be.

It has helped me gain [an] appreciation for women's diverse developmental modes. Now, when I recognize a particular mode in myself or another woman, it can enhance our communication, and help me see and build on our strengths.

Changing Perspectives

Hearing the different perspectives on issues from women in different age groups opened my eyes quite a bit. . . . I now feel I have some intellectual backup to the way I feel as a woman and the way society treats women. . . . Now I've entered a whole new phase in terms of understanding my beliefs, attitudes, and values.

This course has opened my eyes to the fact that women are treated as . . . lesser [individuals] in so many ways that I had over [the] years learned to tune out. I find my hearing to be so much more attuned on these issues.

Being able to explore the meaning of a topic really did change my life. So often I feel I'm just going through the motions of the transitions I'm in, without analyzing the impact it is having on my life or fully appreciating the growth and development that is taking place.

Empowering Oneself

In these past ten weeks, I have ended an unhealthy relationship and am finally standing up for myself, against all odds, when persons were trying to knock me down.

This course has been a useful tool for me to use in developing my skills to handle things differently, as well as [to handle] stressful situations.

It made me realize that I can change things about myself.

Seeking Growth and Development

Since I understand more now how to handle transitions, I will encourage myself to grow and change in whatever direction feels right. I will not stand in the way of new learning or new experiences that would expand my mind and the way to view things. I definitely want more for myself intellectually than I have today, so I will plunge ahead in order to keep changing and growing and hope the cycle continues for the rest of my life. . . . I am not afraid anymore of plunging into the unknown; rather, I welcome the challenges that are ahead.

Ideally, I would like to be able to take a more "proactive" role in producing change in my life, rather than a "reactive" role. Making changes is always risky—but many things can be gained even from change that others may view as negative. Recognizing the power I have to influence change in my own life is a big step towards making change.

Growing is hard sometimes, especially when it requires that we rethink or let go of outmoded ways of thinking or being. But for me, the rewards of moving on are much greater than the comfort of staying in the old pattern.

I now know that I have choices. I feel a new sense of freedom, and I am confident that I will continue to change and grow. I plan to search for what my true inner voice is calling. . . . This is my time now. I can continue on my journey of self-discovery, while still staying connected to those whom I love.

Teaching Women's Development to Developing Women

The overarching theme among these women's voices appears to be a sense of self-discovery. They have found a place to stand from which they can look at their self, and they have learned to find and fashion their own voice. One hears, as well, the basis for the theories that form much of the content of my course Women's Psychosocial Development—that is, female-based and female-inclusive models of development. *Women's Ways of Knowing* (Belenky, Clinchy, Goldberger, and Tarule, 1986) is both the primary text and a means of interpreting what we have heard in the preceding section—the development of "self, voice, and mind" that follows from sensing one's capacity to speak and to know one's own mind. Peck's model (1986) is also central to the course because it "considers the effects of social/historical factors" along with the "importance of caring and relationships" (p. 274), thereby offering a particularly useful framework for a group of diverse women learners to examine the critical factors affecting their knowledge of self. Peck's model and Kegan's description of the major developmental shift of adulthood as the "growth and loss of the interpersonal self" (1982) also help us interpret what the women in my course are saying.

The development of self and of identity and of the self-in-relation are themes that recurred prominently in these women's end-of-course assessments, reflecting the work of Miller (1986), Baruch, Barnett, and Rivers (1983), Kegan (1982), Surrey (1991), Lyons (1988), and Bateson (1989). We also examine the effects of age, race, ethnicity, and class on development through the works of Scott (1991), Anzaldua (1990), Joseph and Lewis (1981), and others. Change and transition as components of the developmental process are understood through Schlossberg (1984) and Bridges (1980). Gilligan (1982) provides a base for examining ethical perspectives, along with Belenky, Clinchy, Goldberger, and Tarule (1986). The male-based works of Perry (1981), Kohlberg (1973), Levinson (1978), and Erikson (1959) are examined briefly, both for contrast to the female-based frameworks studied and for possible relevance to students in thinking about their own development.

The emphasis on female-centered models of development has enabled us—both the women learners in my class and myself—to explore women's development (and some of its differences from men's development) from a positive rather than a defensive posture. We no longer have to study and teach about the ways in which women do not measure up to a "standard." Instead, we listen, as Caffarella and Olson advocate, to "alternative voices of development . . . the voices of women" (1993, p. 126).

Listening to the voices of women is central to my teaching. I want each woman to learn to listen to her own voice, to the voices of other learners and my own, as well as to the voices found in the literature. I want listening to become part of the conversation of learning. Given this aim, I use learners' experiences and perspectives as the point of entry into examining and trying on the various theories and models of development. Learners reflect on their own experiences through a variety of narratives: a structured learning journal (see Chapter Two), freewriting, and individual and group exercises. In addition to conversational exchange, we all tell our stories—I do too—stories that we reflect on, both individually and in groups, and that I then use as a springboard for introducing new concepts and theories. This approach validates learners' experiences and provides a foundation for each of them to make meaning out of complex material. And by integrating their own experiences with the material, they can test the relevance of a given theory or model to their own lives or the lives of other women.

It seems paradoxical: providing women with theoretical frameworks within which to examine their experiences and language with which to articulate their self-discoveries contributes to the very development that such theories and language describe. Jane credits the course for "helping to create a place" for her to "learn with the knowledge that was mine all along." Though not every woman's self-discovery is as stirring, I try to offer each woman the opportunity to connect herself with some aspect of the course material so that she can move forward—not necessarily in big leaps but in the direction of developmental growth. Most seem to find a place in the course material and with one another to explore, reflect on, and change their perspectives of themselves, both as learners and as developing women. It is through our coming together to explore the differences and similarities in our lives as women, to examine our experiences in the context of each other's experiences as well as theories and models, to look inside in order to connect to the outside, that we contribute to significant shifts in our beliefs, attitudes, understandings, and behaviors.

And most women learners do find and fashion their voice. As one woman wrote at the end of the course, "An interesting thing along the way is that once I was able to voice my thoughts, what I thought about something often changed and moved to a higher level. Somehow, being listened to (and hearing my own voice) facilitated that change." It is through the voices of women learners that we can better understand the value of knowing about our own development and the authenticity of the theories highlighted in this sourcebook.

References

Anzaldua, G. (ed.). *Making Face, Making Soul: Creative and Critical Perspectives by Feminists of Color*. San Francisco: Aunt Lute Body, 1990.

Baruch, G., Barnett, R., and Rivers, C. *LifePrints: New Patterns of Love and Work for Today's Women*. New York: Macmillan, 1983.

Bateson, M. C. *Composing a Life*. New York: Atlantic Monthly Press, 1989.

Belenky, M. F., Clinchy, B. M., Goldberger, N. R., and Tarule, J. M. *Women's Ways of Knowing: The Development of Self, Voice, and Mind*. New York: Basic Books, 1986.

Bridges, W. *Transitions: Making Sense of Life's Changes*. Reading, Mass.: Addison-Wesley, 1980.

Caffarella, R., and Olson, S. "Psychosocial Development of Women: A Critical Review of the Literature." *Adult Education Quarterly*, 1993, *43* (1), 125–151.

Erikson, E. H. *Identity and the Life Cycle*. Psychological Issues Monograph 1. New York: International Universities Press, 1959.

Gilligan, C. *In a Different Voice: Psychological Theory and Women's Development*. Cambridge, Mass.: Harvard University Press, 1982.

Joseph, G., and Lewis, J. *Common Differences: Conflicts in Black and White Feminist Perspectives*. Boston: Southend Press, 1981.

Kegan, R. *The Evolving Self: Problem and Process in Human Development*. Cambridge, Mass.: Harvard University Press, 1982.

Kohlberg, L. "Continuities in Childhood and Adult Moral Development Revisited." In P. B. Baltes and K. W. Schaie (eds.), *Life-Span Developmental Psychology: Personality and Socialization*. New York: Academic Press, 1973.

Levinson, D. J., Darrow, C., Kline, E., Levinson, M., and McKee, B. *The Seasons of a Man's Life*. New York: Knopf, 1978.

Lyons, N. P. "Two Perspectives: On Self, Relationships, and Morality." In C. Gilligan, J. V. Ward, and J. M. Taylor (eds.), *Mapping the Moral Domain*. Cambridge, Mass.: Harvard University Press, 1988.

Mezirow, J. *Transformative Dimensions of Adult Learning*. San Francisco: Jossey-Bass, 1991.

Miller, J. B. *Toward a New Psychology of Women*. (2nd ed.) Boston: Beacon Press, 1986.

Peck, T. "Women's Self-Definition in Adulthood: From a Different Model?" *Psychology of Women Quarterly*, 1986, *10*, 274–284.

Perry, W. G., Jr. "Cognitive and Ethical Growth: The Making of Meaning." In A. W. Chickering and Associates, *The Modern American College: Responding to the New Realities of Diverse Students and a Changing Society*. San Francisco: Jossey-Bass, 1981.

Schlossberg, N. *Counseling Adults in Transition*. New York: Springer, 1984.

Scott, K. *The Habit of Surviving: Black Women's Strategies for Life*. New Brunswick, N.J.: Rutgers University Press, 1991.

Surrey, J. "The Self-in-Relation: A Theory of Women's Development." In J. Jordon, A. Kaplan, J. B. Miller, I. Stiver, and J. Surrey, *Women's Growth in Connection*. New York: Guilford Press, 1991.

CATHERINE MARIENAU is associate professor in the School for New Learning at DePaul University and is active in the Alliance (an association for alternative degree programs for adults).

Learning environments and pedagogical strategies can support the development of women of color, nonnative speakers of English, and the economically disadvantaged.

Teaching to the Developmental Needs of Nonmainstream Learners

Linda Gajdusek, Helen Gillotte

Belenky, Clinchy, Goldberger, and Tarule (1986) focus our attention on the concept of voice as a powerful metaphor for women's intellectual development. They also help us to understand the particular challenges to learning and development faced by others who, like women, are not part of the academic mainstream: persons of color, nonnative speakers of English, and the economically disadvantaged. Though these categories obviously include men, and some of the same concerns apply across genders, we will emphasize challenges to nonmainstream women learners.

In situations where men are perceived as dominant, such as the traditional academic classroom, nonnative speakers of English are often too intimidated to risk active participation. Furthermore, for many women for whom English is not their native tongue, particularly those from non-European and underdeveloped countries, their voice may be repressed by cultural patterns that challenge their right—as women—to have a voice. If we are diverted by their more obvious second-language handicap, we may fail to realize the multiple causes of their silence.

This phenomenon is not tied only to language and cultural difference; it is also a matter of color and gender. An African American professor of English reflects on her experience of "the intimidation factor."

> My husband, who is a poet, always talks to me about his work. He listens to me about interpretations, vocabulary, meanings, and so forth. But when we're sitting around the table, and his poetry-writing friends are here and everyone is responding to everyone else's work, I clam up. I don't say anything. I just pull back. And I see this same thing happen with women in my classes all the time.

All of a sudden it's as if "I know nothing." Even though I'm older than my husband, have more degrees—even though I've turned my husband on to poets and authors, I sit back and allow him and his male friends to be the authorities.

If this is the response of a highly educated, professional woman of color, we should not be surprised that women with less cause for self-confidence exhibit a reluctance to speak up (much less speak out) in the academic context. Furthermore, the potential for intimidation is increased when a student is the only person of color or the only person of a particular ethnic group in a classroom. The same professor, reflecting on her experience as a graduate student at a renowned institution, recalled:

I was taking a course from a well-known linguist who was discussing black vernacular English—BVE—with us. As was the case in many of my classes, I was the only black student. Fortunately, I was used to this. But I was not ready for the professor's request. I was asked to speak in BVE. I couldn't believe my ears. It was as if, being black, I must surely have spoken BVE at some time or other. I said, "I'm sorry, I don't know how, I've never spoken BVE."

In such an environment, a student will be silent not only for fear of not having the right answers or of appearing to be uninformed but also as a rejection of the depersonalizing role of classroom representative of her (or his) race, culture, or community.

Being Outside the Mainstream Affects a Woman's Development

It is apparent that a fear of speaking out has a negative effect on a woman's development. In the English as a second language (ESL), developmental studies (DS), and composition classrooms, language is both the content and medium of instruction. As a result, those of us in these disciplines have long been mindful of the way in which the issues of language and voice play out in the intellectual development of women whose primary life experience has been outside that of the American mainstream. Among the factors that can place women out of this mainstream are language and skin color. But because both are such readily identifiable characteristics, they may divert attention from the developmental issues that they simultaneously conceal and aggravate.

Inexperienced writers, for example, regardless of their language backgrounds, often fail to recognize differences between spoken and written language. (As one instance, we hear "suppose to"; we write—in standard English—"supposed to.") While the difference between the sound and the look of words is a significant language usage issue, adequate context and a structure that will satisfy the reader's expectations are characteristics that will have greater impact on the success of the written product. They are also tied to developmental issues. For example, writers in the academy are expected to provide context for readers who may not share the writers' perspective. Also, the culture of the academy, which nonmainstream learners do not even perceive, requires that writers structure their ideas in a rigorous, fairly formulaic sequence. Nonmainstream writers may fail to grasp the importance of supporting their assertions because they do not have the perspective to distinguish between "fact" and "opinion."

Teachers who focus on the more trivial, albeit distracting, language errors may lose sight of the more significant lack of perspective and perception, with the unfortunate result that the more important developmental needs of learners are not addressed.

The teacher's pedagogical agenda may further aggravate the problem. For nonnative speakers, language learning is not just a matter of mastering cognitive content; it is also skill-building. The eventual goal is accurate, automated language use, which—at certain levels of production—we no longer have to consciously control. However, this language skill is only one means to the real end, communication. "Communication competence" (Canale and Swain, 1980) is the goal, and several decades of language learning research and theory have persuaded us that successful language teaching must stimulate learners to actively, meaningfully, and thoughtfully use the target language. So we constantly create challenging, thought-provoking opportunities for learners to use their literal and metaphoric voices—often long before they are developmentally or emotionally prepared to do so.

For many of these same learners, their social roles and cultural reality have not encouraged or permitted them to move into the worlds of the subjective much less the procedural knower (Belenky, Clinchy, Goldberger, and Tarule, 1986). Many have been educated in cultures where the prevailing wisdom is that the nail that sticks up highest will be pounded down first. When this is added to the subordinate role of women in many cultures, we find that the resulting learning strategy is to quietly, passively "receive" knowledge from the all-powerful, all-knowing authority figure of the teacher (of either gender). This is a learning style well suited to cultures where the questioning that is an implicit part of taking personal responsibility might be seen as disruptive of the prevailing cultural norms.

Furthermore, in many cultures the harmony of the group is the paramount social and interpersonal value. This seems a nice enough concept—who does not want harmony? But this very concept has also been used to deny a voice to countless persons—often women—who are told (implicitly and explicitly) to be silent rather than upset the harmony of the group. And this practice is not limited to foreign cultures. The astonishing frequency of spousal and childhood abuse of reentry women is testimony to the fact that many U.S. women have also been taught that if their voices question the prevailing "harmony," they will be punished, or in Archie Bunker's term, "stifled."

Investigating the response of Chinese students to peer-response activities, which are common in many American writing classrooms, Nelson, Carson, Gajdusek, and Danison (in press) found that this type of concern for maintaining the harmony of the group often subverts the instructor's educational goals. For example, as the following excerpts from three students reveal, they would remain silent or find less threatening issues to discuss rather than honestly identify a problem in a partner's text and risk making an overt criticism:

> In China people just hide their thoughts; they don't want to talk about it even if you ask. If the group were in China, they would talk about their essay is very good; everything about the essay is good; they never talk about "Oh, this is wrong; this is not good." They never talk that way. And if I were in China, I would do the same thing because I remember when I talk to my friends, I always say something good.

> It's really hard for me to say that I don't agree. I think if I said something like, "I don't agree with you," it's like I'm really mad at him or her, really angry.

> Argument? Well, I just try to end this argument. . . . If they argue, if it's very serious, I'll hide myself. I think it's very terrible.

Strategies That Build Developmental Bridges

While some observers might conclude that educators should therefore abandon peer critiques and interactions, we would rather aim to understand and acknowledge the concerns of these learners so we can actively address them and thereby meet, rather than ignore, these students' developmental needs.

Many students from cultural backgrounds outside the mainstream feel overwhelmed when they confront not only a new and intimidating language but also a new and equally intimidating teaching style. On the one hand, what our students learn as they encounter new modes of thought in the classroom does move them along the ladder of intellectual development, as the authors of *Women's Ways of Knowing* (Belenky, Clinchy, Goldberger, and Tarule, 1986) define it. On the other hand, many students from nonmainstream backgrounds are painfully frustrated when they confront a teaching style that requires their active participation not only in the production of English at a basic level but also in the active processing of their own ideas and attitudes.

One strategy is to involve learners in an examination of assumptions that produce counterproductive results. For example, we help both men and women examine their tacit assumptions about "harmony" and the "appropriate" (that is, acquiescent and silent) role of women, in light of their needs as learners. We may then encourage discussion of strategies for resolving conflict between their academic goals and long-held cultural beliefs. Finally, we model the language and strategies of successful critical interaction, providing learners with ample opportunity to practice these skills. Ultimately students see that it is okay to have and appropriately express an opinion, even when it is different or critical. These experiences can be essential first steps to developmental growth.

In addition to modeling the appropriate academic behavior and the language to facilitate critical thought, we also attempt to create the needed security—what Kegan calls a "holding environment" (1982)—to permit the risk that growth entails. A composition professor describes "scaffolding," a term she borrows from Applebee and Langer (1982), as one instructional method for providing this security.

> [Scaffolding] empowers students with their own authority. You take a task you want them to accomplish and then build a scaffold, a structure, for them, like a stepladder, which they can move up. And you work with them to see they have accomplished the first step and then move them along to the next until they complete the task. Not only do they complete it, but in such a way that you are no longer needed as their teacher. Then you begin to facilitate—so that they rely more and more on their own accomplishments. Finally, you can give them another task, and now they have a scaffold they can use to do their own learning. This works especially well with students of color who have never done any kind of writing before.

The instructor's role in creating an effective developmental bridge or scaffold is crucial. In the case of peer-group work, the teacher may initially need to join the group and provide the security (the holding environment) of a benign authority figure for learners who are insecure not only with the intimidating academic language but also with the demand that they take an active role in the learning process. However, although this figure participates with the group, he or she does not do the work for the group. Rather, the teacher participant's role is to model appropriate responses, deflect inappropriate ones, and provide safety, encouragement, and recognition of desired behaviors when they do occur. This solution may be more time consuming for the teacher, who must be present (at least at the beginning, until the learners start to master the goals and forms), but it is one way to bridge cultural chasms and engage learners from their developmental starting points. This type of direct participation helps students construct the connection they need to move out of the isolation their culture and learning styles may have placed them in.

The challenge for those of us who work with nonmainstream learners in ESL, DS, and composition classes is to develop a variety of such teaching practices, to provide learners with the confidence they need to engage in the active production of language and thus achieve important educational and language proficiency goals. Without conscious awareness of the effect on development, many teachers of nonmainstream learners have successfully adopted teaching practices that also encourage women to find their voice. These are a few of the techniques we have used that provide this additional benefit:

- We model the intellectual or linguistic behavior we want our students to learn, and then we create opportunities for the students to practice it themselves while we provide immediate feedback. We use sample essays written by former students in response to a given task (the task that we will shortly be assigning or that we have just assigned) to model the desired form and product. We encourage class members to analyze the model text for its strengths and weaknesses. We also use texts generated by students in the class, often working with transparencies to model and facilitate analysis and revision.

In more traditional classrooms, assignments take the form of an abstract description of an expected product. Nonmainstream learners are often frustrated by this approach because their previous experience does not help them imagine what the expected product should look like, nor does it give them confidence that they have the skills needed to produce it. In fact they have many relevant skills; this alternative way of presenting a task (inviting, even modeling, students' evaluative interaction with a potential product) demonstrates how to use these skills and creates confidence in their ability to build on their prior experience to achieve new learning.

• We actively teach critical thinking—modeling it, providing specific examples of it, and making explicit the critical attitude that asks questions as well as the appropriate language for asking them. For example, as we interact with a text and solve the problems that it raises, we move from literal questions that establish the "facts" (for example, "When was Lincoln assassinated?") to more interpretive questions ("What was the effect of Lincoln's death on the outcome of Reconstruction?") to the even more difficult questions that require awareness of the writer's rhetorical purpose:

Q: What is the "function" of paragraph one?
A: It introduces the topic of Lincoln's assassination.
Q: Yes, but *how* does it introduce the topic? Does it describe it? Does it define it? Does it evaluate it?

The last set of questions demands a metacognitive awareness—not of content but of the way language functions regardless of the content. The movement from understanding content (facts), through increasingly abstract interpretation, and finally to an abstract, metacognitive awareness of the way language itself operates is a developmental movement—one that, again, ties new kinds of learning to concepts that have already been acquired. Belenky, Clinchy, Goldberger, and Tarule (1986) remind us that learners must first master the necessary intellectual tools and formulas if they are to achieve social and psychological growth. These same tools are the ones that will permit them to function at the level of abstraction that academic tasks take as a given.

This development of a metacognitive awareness of language is similar to the transition from third- to fourth-order consciousness described in Kegan's model (1994); that is, a transition from an embeddedness in and absolute identification with the psychological surround to a distance from which it is possible to observe, question, and challenge one's rules of perception and interpretation (see Chapters One, Three, and Ten).

• We require that learners take responsibility for the form as well as the content of the work they submit—that they edit and evaluate their own work.

Too many of our students have inferred from previous teaching practices that it is the job of the teacher, the figure in authority, to edit (correct) and evaluate what they produce. Consequently, these students have become passive students, not active learners who take responsibility for the whole product.

• We rely on journals as an important course component. Journals provide a safe place where students can begin to shape their ideas in a private setting. Journals give students an opportunity to unveil their feelings and to explore personal, sometimes tentative responses to ideas that the teacher can validate, helping the student gain a sense of worth and, one hopes, the courage to engage more openly in class discussion. (Chapter Two explores this territory more thoroughly.)

• We assign group work (sometimes in a peer-response situation, as discussed earlier) and collaborative work to help shift the responsibility for discovering and creating knowledge from the teacher back to groups and individual learners. As an active-productive rather than a passive-receptive mode, group work provides an opportunity for active learner involvement, which in turn helps develop self-confidence and even leadership potential.

But of all the strategies we employ to address the needs of nonmainstream learners, group work presents the most potential difficulty for women, especially in a cross-cultural context. While many of the expectations concerning communication in the traditional classroom are daunting enough to nonmainstream learners, the situation for nonmainstream women is further complicated by gender roles. For example, women in small groups may face the additional burden of the more competitive, dominating, and, at least superficially, self-confident behavior of some (it only takes one) men in the group. In short, these women may be disadvantaged several times over: by language, by skin color, by economic status, by a lack of access to the forms of academic discourse, and by gender.

The point is not to abandon developmentally encouraging strategies that rely on dialogue, interaction, and different sorts of group work but to examine the contradictions and problems associated with learner-centered education—for example, the group learning configuration—so that we can consciously make our teaching choices sensitive to the needs of learners while they also reflect the goals we are trying to achieve.

Conclusion

In articulating some special needs of nonmainstream learners and approaches to teaching them, we accomplish a double goal. First, we raise the consciousness of instructors about potential conflicts between the cultural patterns and developmental needs of nonmainstream learners, whose numbers are increasing in the reentry population on our campuses. In addition, the experiences of these learners bring into bold relief certain patterns, problems, and needs of reentry women in general—women who have been marginalized by, if not excluded from, the mainstream. The solutions that we develop to meet the needs of women of color and ESL learners may well serve the developmental needs of a much wider range of reentry women.

References

Applebee, A., and Langer, J. "Moving Toward Excellence: Writing and Learning in Secondary School Curriculum." Proposal to the National Institutes of Education, Stanford University, Stanford, Calif., 1982.

Belenky, M. F., Clinchy, B. M., Goldberger, N. R., and Tarule, J. M. *Women's Ways of Knowing: The Development of Self, Voice, and Mind.* New York: Basic Books, 1986.

Canale, M., and Swain, M. "Theoretical Bases of Communicative Approaches to Second Language Teaching and Testing." *Applied Linguistics,* 1980, *1,* 1–47.

Kegan, R. *The Evolving Self: Problem and Process in Human Development.* Cambridge, Mass.: Harvard University Press, 1982.

Kegan, R. *In Over Our Heads: The Mental Demands of Modern Life.* Cambridge, Mass.: Harvard University Press, 1994.

Nelson, G., Carson, J., Gajdusek, L., and Danison, N. "Social Dimensions of Second Language Writing Instruction: Peer Response Groups as Cultural Context." In D. Rubin (ed.), *Identity and Style in Written Language.* Hillsdale, N.J.: Erlbaum, in press.

LINDA GAJDUSEK *is assistant professor of applied linguistics and ESL and assistant director of the Intensive ESL program at Georgia State University. She has taught English to native and nonnative speakers of English since 1964.*

HELEN GILLOTTE *is associate professor of English and coordinator of reading at San Francisco State University and co-coordinator of the Bay Area K–16 Educational Collaborative.*

Women's Ways of Knowing provides the theoretical framework for a core curriculum designed to meet the learning needs of women.

A Developmental Core Curriculum for Adult Women Learners

Rosemarie Carfagna

What might a core curriculum look like that takes the learning needs of women seriously and maximizes their potential for personal development and social leadership? This is an increasingly urgent and important question today, particularly for women's colleges. Based on my experience at Ursuline College in Ohio, I know that the returning adult woman approaches a women's college with these concerns:

> I've raised a family and held a responsible job for the past twenty years. Now coming back to school is something I'm doing for me. Are you willing to meet me halfway and treat me as an equal?

> I've been at home with my small children so long I'm afraid my brain is turning to mush. Do you think I can survive in a college classroom? It's been a long time.

> I can't advance in my career without the right credentials. Does what you have to offer here relate to my plans for a professional future? Will this program be anything more than jumping through a set of hoops to get what I really deserve anyway?

Our faculty heard these kinds of questions, and the expectations and concerns embedded in them, throughout the 1970s and 1980s. The influx of returning women to the college—two-thirds of the student population of 1,600 are adult learners—triggered a curriculum change that transformed virtually our entire campus. In a revision of the college's mission statement in the mid 1980s, our faculty unanimously affirmed the college's commitment to

NEW DIRECTIONS FOR ADULT AND CONTINUING EDUCATION, no. 65, Spring 1995 © Jossey-Bass Publishers

women's education and called for a curriculum that would address the issues and opportunities facing women in that decade and beyond.

Women as Learners

In undertaking the curriculum revision, faculty members turned to the literature on educational philosophy, learning theory, and human development for guidance. We found relevant thinking in Dewey (1938), Freire (1970), and Perry (1981)—the latter particularly because of his balanced emphasis on cognitive and ethical development during the college years. But it was *Women's Ways of Knowing* (Belenky, Clinchy, Goldberger, and Tarule, 1986) that emerged as the most influential source, in large part because the voices of the women in the book closely matched the voices and experiences of students on Ursuline's campus. Those voices include the strong, successful career woman and mother of grown children who senses a need to expand and deepen her own education but definitely on her own terms; the young mom whose life has revolved around small children to the point that she doubts her ability to tackle serious academic work; the entry-level professional who returns to school for purely pragmatic reasons, but who may hope inwardly that school has something more to offer her than a promotion or a raise.

The authors of *Women's Ways of Knowing* gathered the results of 135 interviews with women of diverse ages and life experiences; these interviews revealed what the authors describe as five epistemological positions, or ways of knowing: silence, received knowing, subjective knowing, procedural knowing, and constructed knowing. These positions represent an intellectual continuum; the extent to which they represent sequential or hierarchical positions of development remains open to question. The five positions, or perspectives on knowing, are described briefly here.

Silence. Silent women have little experience and awareness of self. They believe that knowledge is wholly external, possessed by those in authority (for example, teachers, employers, spouses), and they see themselves as obedient to and dependent upon these powerful figures. It does not occur to a silent woman that she should or could think for herself. Given the depth of their voicelessness, truly silent women are seldom found in higher education. Many other women can, however, recall the experience of feeling silent in the classroom. As one returning Ursuline student said, "I didn't say anything in class. I never spoke, or at least I didn't want to. I felt very intimidated. There were a lot of people in the class. So I just kept my mouth shut."

Received knowing. Received knowers see themselves as careful listeners to the ideas, thoughts, and convictions of others who know more than they do. They see those in authority as infallible possessors of the truth. Their notion of knowledge is the accurate recording and faithful recitation of what someone in authority tells them is true. Their concept of self is closely linked to the approval and affirmation of authorities. As students, women who are received knowers take good notes, memorize well, and do well on objective tests. Their stance is that knowledge is objective, concrete, factual, known by experts, and not within their jurisdiction to create. One woman learner at Ursuline described received knowing this way: "I think you're going to stick more with what the teacher thinks, just because you know when the test comes, they're going to go by what they said. They are the right ones."

Subjective knowing. Subjective knowers have a much stronger sense of self than silent or received knowers. They are aware of their own ideas, thoughts, and convictions, and they are able to express them with a certain degree of confidence. Their knowledge is gained from personal experience, and they take the words of authorities with a grain of salt. They see the truth as personal and make value decisions based primarily upon their own convictions or instincts. Traditional education has placed very little value on subjective knowing. However, this is the kind of knowing at which returning adult students tend to excel, and they expect their experiences and views to be respected and valued in the classroom. When given the opportunity to express their subjective voice, women learners at Ursuline relish the adventure: "Finding my own individual beliefs and values has been a big part of my life for the past six years. I learned by trial and tribulation." "Can't nobody make a decision for you about what you are going to learn. Cause you have that choice; even if they present the material to you, if you don't like it and that's not what you want, you are not going to get it anyway." "I'm really an outspoken person. I believe that what I have to say is important. Whether it is or whether it isn't doesn't matter to me. I only know that it's my opinion."

Procedural knowing. Educators recognize that admirable and necessary as subjective knowing is, it cannot be an end in itself. To be credible members of the academic community, students need to develop a procedural kind of knowing in which they learn either to step outside their own experience to consider others or to harmonize their voice with the voices of others. Procedural knowers, having established a stronger sense of identity, self-confidence, and self-esteem, are capable of listening to peers and authorities with interest. They are able to look at knowledge from a variety of perspectives, and they value experiences different from their own. Procedural knowers can work comfortably within the frameworks (or "procedures") of a variety of academic disciplines: in philosophy they can use the rules of logic; in an art class they can employ principles of artistic criticism; in a history class they can deal effectively with primary sources; in a literature class they can analyze a work using the principles of literary criticism.

Traditional education values a *separate* style of procedural knowing, in which the rules of various disciplines become weapons for competition among scholars and lead to ever more esoteric and specialized investigations. Though some women are drawn to separate knowing, most are more comfortable with a *connected* style of procedural knowing, in which communication with peers, teachers, and experts is characterized by cooperation rather than competition. Whereas separate knowing may be seen as critical thinking, which seeks to find flaws in another's perspective, connected knowing might be termed appreciative thinking, which seeks to understand and "get inside" another's perspective. Connected procedural knowers also value an interdisciplinary approach to study, where connections among disciplines mirror connections among students and among various cultures and historical periods. When commenting on this style of knowing, one student said, "Now I think about things more. I can see a pattern, a change in my pattern of thinking. And because I think more, I think I'm becoming more aware of things." Another student said, "I think I've become more objective. I look at other peoples' points of view. I used to be kind of narrow-minded, and now I see the whole spectrum of things."

Constructed knowing. Constructed knowers view themselves and their world in holistic terms. They value both subjective and objective strategies for knowing. Constructed knowers have a good sense of self and form comfortable working relationships with a variety of peers and teachers. They view knowledge as contextual and see themselves as capable of generating new knowledge in concert with others, including experts in various fields. Constructed knowers are also ready to apply what they know to real-life contexts, particularly in collaborative problem solving.

While higher education implicitly aims at constructed knowing, traditionally it has neglected the developmental processes needed to create constructed knowers. Too often it has settled for producing graduates who have diplomas but not education, people who are masters of information who can compete and win but who cannot work with others or make practical applications of what they have learned. By contrast, constructed knowers value connections and applications. Listen to two of the Ursuline women's voices:

> I did receive a syllabus, but what's so comfortable about this class is that it made me feel that I am going to take from it everything that the instructors expect me to learn, but I also am going to apply my learning. I am going to make a decision as to how I could take what I've learned from that class and apply it somewhere else.

> I learned to observe people and treat them how I wanted to be treated. That has helped me a lot because I was the kind of person who would do what I wanted to do. Now I find you have to work with people more to accomplish what everyone wants and not just do what you want to do.

In keeping with the theoretical framework of *Women's Ways of Knowing,* Ursuline's faculty hypothesized that as women develop, they change their positions toward self, authority, truth, and voice. They seem to progress from a position of silence in which they are unable to express their own ideas or convictions to one of received knowing, in which they attribute ideas and convictions to experts and authorities outside themselves. An important shift occurs when they move to subjective knowing, in which they firmly establish their own identity, self-confidence, and self-esteem as learners. Having accomplished that developmental task, they may go on to investigate and internalize a wide variety of opinions and experiences that are different from their own, including the work of experts in academic disciplines (procedural knowing). Finally, they may arrive at a learning stance in which they creatively integrate their own knowledge and experience with that of others and make something new out of it for themselves and society (constructed knowing.)

Given that the *Women's Ways of Knowing* schema matched the faculty's perception of actual student development and learning, it offered a promising framework for radically transforming the core curriculum. The Ursuline faculty did acknowledge two drawbacks to the schema: it is hypothetical, and it can appear to be lockstep at first. Nevertheless, the faculty agreed that its stages of developmental progression represented valid and desirable academic growth. As a theoretical framework, it provided a coherent way of organizing what previously had been a random set of graduation requirements into a meaningfully arranged core curriculum.

A Core Curriculum for Women

The result of the faculty's study and deliberation was the Ursuline Studies Program, initiated in the fall 1991 semester. This core curriculum approaches the cognitive and ethical development of women through a required series of fourteen courses, totalling forty-nine credit hours, arranged in a coherent sequence to promote student growth. The curriculum balances academic and developmental goals by involving faculty members and student services personnel in a concerted effort to enhance the college experience for returning adult women.

Three courses serve as anchors for the core curriculum: Introductory Seminar, Introduction to Culture, and Culminating Seminar. These courses are designed explicitly to address developmental issues within the epistemological framework of *Women's Ways of Knowing*, as described below.

Introductory Seminar. The Introductory Seminar and four satellite courses drawn from our subject areas of science, math, society, and self form the first cluster of courses in the core curriculum. The aim of the seminar, which is also reflected in the satellite courses, is to help women learners move beyond received knowing (or silence, if necessary) to subjective knowing, and to assist them in the recognition and expression of their personal voice.

The Introductory Seminar was designed collaboratively by faculty members and student services personnel to provide support and challenge to returning adult women. The major themes of the seminar—identity, education, meaning, and voice—are uniquely adapted for two age-specific cohorts: eighteen-to-twenty-two-year-olds and twenty-three-year-olds and older. (This division respects the markedly different levels of experience between the two age groups.) The emphasis on these four themes was influenced by two other important works—Gilligan's *In a Different Voice* (1982) and the American Association of University Women (AAUW) report *How Schools Short-Change Girls*

(1992)—which highlight the pervasive neglect of women's experience and women's voices in traditional education.

Gilligan's poignant description of women without voices motivated the Ursuline faculty to include the achievement of personal voice as a key goal at an early point in the curriculum. The AAUW report's documentation of the dramatic loss of identity, self-confidence, and self-esteem in girls from junior high school through college alerted the faculty to the need to confront these issues directly and to strengthen students, if need be, in these areas before embarking on more traditional academic study.

The faculty recognized that women learn better in climates of cooperation rather than competition. Considerable attention is given to engaging students in collaborative learning activities in the Introductory Seminar. Collaborative learning is supported by small classes (maximum of thirty-two students) in which the strategy of group work—in pairs and small groups of five—is used regularly. Also, faculty members model collaboration through their shared yet distinct roles: while one faculty member facilitates student learning, another attends to student development goals.

Students unfailingly report that the Introductory Seminar facilitates a graceful transition to college life, that it strengthens their self-confidence, and that it provides numerous opportunities for establishing positive, supportive relationships with peers and instructors. Upon completing the course, one woman learner said:

> In four short months, I have grown by leaps and bounds. I don't even recognize the person I was when I started here. I was certain, at that time, that I would need some long-term professional counseling and therapy to put my life back in order. It would have taken years, if I had chosen that route. Instead, I have [faculty members] Ann and Marge to thank for helping me pick up the pieces of my life so I could move on.

Another woman said that the Introductory Seminar helped her find and express herself in her own voice.

> In spite of all my struggles, or perhaps because of them, I have grown this year as an intelligent, hardworking, independent woman. This is an accomplishment of which I am very proud.

Introduction to Culture. The cluster of courses for the next stage of the Ursuline Studies Program includes the anchor course—Introduction to Culture—and four satellite courses, drawn from the areas of world culture, Western culture, American culture, and fine arts. The overall purpose of this cluster of courses is to move students from subjective to procedural knowing, which is characterized by openness to and critical analysis of a wide variety of perspectives that are different from one's own. A related purpose of this cluster, then, is to expose students to personal and cultural diversity.

To support diversity, a wide assortment of courses are available, such as American Music, Religious Traditions of the East, European Theater, and Hispanics in the United States. Students are also exposed to a rich diversity of cultures over time. They explore Athens during the time of Socrates, Florence during the Renaissance, Kyo (the early name for Kyoto, Japan) during the Heian period, Paris during the Enlightenment, and New York City during the 1920s, including the Harlem Renaissance. For each of these cities, students research the art, music, drama, history, literature, philosophy, religion, politics, and daily life that shaped the culture. They also investigate the roles of women in each society, comparing them with their own lives.

The Introduction to Culture stage of the curriculum promotes procedural knowing through the integration of many academic disciplines, synthesis of insights from a variety of cultures, and the ability to function as a peer researcher. In a collaborative learning mode, groups engage in research and are pushed to practice analytical and critical thinking skills that go beyond their reflecting on personal experiences. In addition to providing peer support, the group helps its members focus on developing their skills of critical inquiry. This represents a significant development beyond the important but preliminary position of subjective knowing. One student described this shift in her interview.

> What is most important to me is the continued excitement that began last year with the discovery of myself, and that continues now with the discovery of historical legacies of past cultures that influence my humanity and my heritage. Equally important is being stimulated by the class and the course materials to the point that I want to find the answers to more questions.

Culminating Seminar. The cluster of courses in the third stage of the core curriculum includes the anchor course—the Culminating Seminar—and courses in religious studies and philosophy, which help students focus on their value systems and prepare them to make personal commitments. For example, courses might include spirituality and the helping professions together with women philosophers, or peace and justice together with Existentialism.

The Culminating Seminar, taken as close to graduation as possible, is designed to assist learners to move beyond procedural knowing, emphasized in the second stage of the curriculum, to constructed knowing. Constructed knowing suggests that learners are now able to integrate their own learning with that of others, and that they are able to work with others to create new knowledge to apply to practical problems in meaningful ways.

In the Culminating Seminar, women learners address these questions: "Now that you are completing your college education, what are you going to do with it?" "How will society be better because of what you have learned?" "What difference do you plan to make?" Learners are stimulated to respond to these questions in terms of seminar topics and themes highlighting values and social responsibility, such as women and justice, values in film, and women's autobiographies. Students are also asked to reflect critically upon their learning in relation to goals they set for themselves in the Introductory Seminar, and they then set further goals for their personal and professional futures.

Because the Culminating Seminar is designed to promote constructed knowing, learners find it one of the most personally challenging courses in the curriculum. Far more often than not, however, they are ready for the challenge. For example, one student summarized her experience this way:

> Each of us has an inner voice, and we should follow what it tells us. When we don't follow it, we are unhappy. All of our contributions, whether they be tangible or intangible, give meaning to our lives and reflect our values.

Conclusion

Ursuline's core curriculum enables women to make their inner voices public voices with increasing grace and confidence. The theoretical framework in *Women's Ways of Knowing* has helped the faculty develop a unified sense of direction and purpose for the program while remaining open to its evolution in response to the needs of real students. Ursuline faculty are committed to finding out how well the core curriculum helps women learners move on in terms of their cognitive and ethical growth. A ten-year longitudinal study, begun in 1992, is being conducted that involves surveying 250 students and interviewing another 60 students at regular intervals, starting at the beginning of their program and continuing throughout their time at Ursuline and for five years after graduation. Key questions shaping the longitudinal study include the following: What student qualities promote or hinder development? Which groups of students advance furthest along the theoretical continuum, and why? What aspects of the learning environment promote or hinder student development?

The inauguration and implementation of the Ursuline Studies Program is a bold project. Students welcome its emphasis on their growth and on the achievement of their goals. Faculty members welcome it as a chance to rethink courses and curriculum in new and creative ways, and as a chance to work collaboratively with colleagues for the benefit of the students and faculty alike. The institution welcomes it as a sign of adaptability, strength, and commitment to move women's education into the next century in a way that is academically sound and personally meaningful for everyone involved.

References

American Association of University Women. *The AAUW Report: How Schools Short-Change Girls.* Washington, D.C.: American Association of University Women, 1992.

Belenky, M. F., Clinchy, B. M., Goldberger, N. R., and Tarule, J. M. *Women's Ways of Knowing: The Development of Self, Voice, and Mind.* New York: Basic Books, 1986.

Dewey, J. *Education and Experience.* New York: Collier, 1938.

Freire, P. *Pedagogy of the Oppressed.* New York: Continuum, 1970.

Gilligan, C. *In a Different Voice: Psychological Theory and Women's Development.* Cambridge, Mass.: Harvard University Press, 1982.

Perry, W. G., Jr. "Cognitive and Ethical Growth: The Making of Meaning." In A. W. Chickering and Associates, *The Modern American College: Responding to the New Realities of Diverse Students and a Changing Society.* San Francisco: Jossey-Bass, 1981.

ROSEMARIE CARFAGNA is associate professor of philosophy and religious studies at Ursuline College, where she directs the Ursuline Studies Program. She is involved in research and writing on women and higher education.

Mentors' multiple caring roles with learners can be instrumental in women's growth and development.

Multiple Roles of the Mentor Supporting Women's Adult Development

Mayra Bloom

> When the aim of education is understood to be the *development* of the whole person—rather than knowledge acquisition, for instance—the central element of good teaching becomes the provision of care.
> —Laurent Daloz (1986, p. xvii)

> Mentors do not only care *about* their students; they also care *for* them by making an effort to understand their experience. Apprehending the other's reality, feeling what he feels as nearly as possible, is the essential part of caring. . . . For if I take on the other's reality as possibility and begin to feel its reality, I feel, also, that I must act accordingly; that is, I am impelled to act as though in my own behalf, but in behalf of the other.
> —Nel Noddings (1984, p. 16)

Mentors act on students' behalf, carrying out a myriad of roles and functions; they stand in different relationships to students at different points in the edu-

---

I thank those who shared their experience of mentoring with me and allowed me to include their words here: Sandra Barty, Margaret Blanchard, Felix Carrion, Jim Case, David Fichter, Wendy Goulston, Virginia Holmes, Rhoda Linton, Barbara Marantz, Elizabeth Minnich, Brooke Portman, Mary Priniski, Debra Schultz, and Gail Wheeler.

cational process. At times, for example, the mentor stands *behind* the student, providing what Kegan (1982) calls a "holding environment." At other times the mentor walks a little *ahead* of the learner, functioning, as Daloz (1986) suggests, as a guide. Much—perhaps most—of the time, the mentor engages the student *face-to-face* by listening, questioning, and connecting. Finally, the mentor stands *beside* the student, shoulder to shoulder, offering herself as companion, ally, and sister learner. Underlying all of these relationships, however, is the assumption that human learning and development are rooted in relationships. Drawing on conversations and informal interviews conducted in January 1994 with graduate and undergraduate mentors and learners, this chapter examines how mentors stand in these different relationships to students at different points in the educational process.

Standing Behind the Student: The Mentor and the Holding Environment

One mentor provided a visual image for standing behind the student when she described an outstanding ski instructor.

> He was the only teacher I ever had who skied *behind* me. From that vantage point, he could see everything clearly—strengths as well as weaknesses. He was able to provide accurate, precise, helpful coaching while allowing me to set my own pace. For me, this has remained a metaphor for excellent teaching.

According to Kegan (1982, 1994), development consists of a series of emergences from (and newly formed relationships with) successive "cultures of embeddedness"—families, schools, institutions, mentors. In order to foster an individual's growth, these constituents of the psychological surround must fulfill three basic functions: they must hold on, let go, and remain in place.

A mentor *holds* the reentry woman by accepting her as she is, by designing studies appropriate to her current stage of development (Taylor, 1994), and by seeing her "in the most favorable light consistent with reality" (Noddings, 1984, p. 193). Two mentors use similar metaphors to describe how they hold their learners: one says, "I work from the assumption that whatever I respond to is already within the student; my job is to develop my own ability to draw it out." The other says, "I try to create a container for students to do their own thinking, conveying a quality of attentiveness without invasiveness."

Students often respond with a sense of freedom, relief, and confidence. As two students put it:

> It was freeing to realize that I didn't have to fit into traditional categories. In a sense, I was being reassured that I was OK; my mentor affirmed the way I did what I did.

> My mentor doesn't talk a lot or fill my head with her ideas; she knows how to be in the background, but she has a real presence. Her timing is great; she gives me

room to grow. Sometimes just a phrase or a group of words will stay with me and have a shaping effect. I've learned to really pay attention to what she says.

At the same time as the mentor holds the student, she or he must be prepared to *let go,* or as Kegan puts it, to "assist in the [student's] timely differentiation" (1982, p. 127). To accomplish this, the mentor refrains (as far as possible) from imposing her or his own biases, learning style, or projects on the student, instead encouraging her to find her own way. As one student expressed it:

> The critical thing is that [the mentor] listened to *me,* the learner. She brought her own stuff to our relationship, but she didn't impose it on me. She listened to what I wanted to do and what I was struggling with, and reflected it back to me in a critical, validating, wonderful way. She had a philosophical and practical ability to see what I was doing and [to] transform it to another level, but it was still *me.*

Finally, the mentor must *remain in place* and provide a kind of dynamic constancy as she preserves the memory of how far and in what directions the student has traveled. The mentor, like Penelope, preserves the hearth while the student, like Odysseus, embarks on her own heroic journey. The mentor may sometimes serve as the keeper of the student's deepest commitments, even— or especially—when the student loses sight of them. This can happen in small ways over the course of a single session; as one mentor observed: "I have my antenna out for key questions and words. I listen to the student's first few responses because these are seeds to which I spiral back again and again. As they discuss their own experiences, I often see my role as pulling them back to their opening statements."

As one learner describes it, the mentor may also play a role in keeping commitments in a larger and more profound way.

> Twenty years ago, I had told a professor whom I respected that I wanted to do my master's on "The Self Through Literature." When he said, "That's such a misuse of literature," I immediately capitulated and said, "You're right; that's stupid and wrong," and I did a traditional program instead. Twenty years later, I needed to reclaim the original journey, and with my mentor's help, I've been able to do it. She has helped me stay true to my abiding academic and personal commitments, even when I've forgotten them. It's both whole and soul-making. I know that somebody heard me way back when and remembered. It allows me to say, "I am who I say I am." I haven't lost it; I haven't gone off the deep end. All I care about is integrated in this deep work.

Leading the Student: The Mentor as Guide

Laurent Daloz, author of *Effective Teaching and Mentoring* (1986), sees education as a transformational journey in which mentors act as guides: "They embody our hopes, cast light on the way ahead, interpret arcane signs, warn us of lurking dangers, and point out unexpected delights along the way" (p. 177).

According to Daloz, mentors can be trusted because they have been there—they have learned from and can draw upon their experience. As one learner points out, however, the territory may be as unfamiliar to the guide as it is to the follower: "Guides don't necessarily know the terrain better than anyone else; what they do have are the skills to survive once you're out there."

Daloz points out that, in their capacity as guides, mentors express care for students by engendering trust, issuing challenges, providing encouragement, and offering visions for the journey (p. 30). As a mentor, I have discovered, for example, that many reentry women experience—and must learn to tolerate— periods of anxiety, ambiguity, and even chaos before their educational goals become clear. I have also seen that for most students there comes a moment of clarity, of crystallization, when their programs suddenly fall into place and they—and I—realize where they have been headed all along. A learner describes the process vividly:

> My mentor often let me flounder around. At the time, I would get very frus-
> trated. Now when I look back, I say, "Thank you," because if she had been
> quicker to rescue me, there wouldn't have been as much learning. She allowed
> the frustration so that the work that finally emerged would be mine, not hers.

The confidence required to let a student flounder comes with experience, as does knowledge of particular educational systems, access to resources, and competence in identifying areas of potential life experience credit. In these areas, certainly, the mentor functions as a guide.

Face-to-Face: The Mentor as Listener, Questioner, Connector

It is significant that we have begun to think of women's development in terms of voice (Belenky, Clinchy, Goldberger, and Tarule, 1986; Gilligan, 1982). In traditional settings, it is the teacher's voice that drives the educational process; the students are there to absorb and parrot back what they have heard. In contrast, mentors are concerned with the development of the student's voice, and they facilitate this development by listening. It is primarily through listening that the mentor gains access to the learner's experience, which according to Noddings (1984) is the basis of caring. To the developing reentry woman, who despite her accomplishments often feels like an imposter in the academic world (McIntosh, 1985), being heard confirms that she has something valuable to say and that her voice deserves to be heard. As one student wrote to her mentor:

> I'd never have had the nerve to share any of the thoughts I've shared with you—
> especially those that show that I take myself seriously. But you make people feel

that you take seriously what they care to think about, and you take the fact that they care to think even more seriously.

In reviewing ways in which mentors support their students' development, Daloz (1986) also starts with listening: "We can listen to our students' stories, seeking to understand how their quest for education fits into the larger questions and movements of their lives" (p. xviii). But at the same time that the mentor listens *to* a student's story, she also listens *through* the words in order to discern the patterns, characteristics, and structures of the student's thought. According to Elizabeth Minnich, author of *Transforming Knowledge* (1990) and a mentor in a nontraditional doctoral program, this kind of listening often follows a pattern of taking in, retrieving, and reflecting.

In a 1994 conversation with me for this chapter, Minnich described the mentor's first crucial step as simply taking in the student's words and presence and refraining from giving an immediate response—even if the student wants one:

> The real need is to be what Simone Weil called "attentive"; trying, precisely, *not* to meet what you're hearing with categories. Categories do not come first; experience comes first. Categories should be used to check things out or point in particular directions. But first, you participate, you join. The first movement is that of going quiet, going in.

At the same time that the mentor is listening—without judgment or premature categorization—he or she may become aware of images or metaphors that arise without invitation. In Minnich's words:

> What happens is that you begin to "find yourself with" the student. You may see an almost visual mapping of the form of someone's thought; you get a picture, for example, of the person piling thought upon thought as if she were building a building. Or you may see that she works from a central insight, weaving in and out of it in a process of articulating and unfolding that central idea. Or you say to yourself, "This person is always working between two apparent opposites. On the one hand, she is always speaking about structure, logic, and proof. On the other hand, she is always making connections and focusing on interrelationships—which seems, on the face of it, to be a contradiction."

As Minnich describes it, listening is not simply a cognitive process. Being attentive involves one's entire body—one's entire being:

> When you listen attentively, you sense by the end that you know the person better; if someone asks how you got that sense, the culture points us toward the content of what she or he said. Actually this is only a small—perhaps the smallest—part. You are also listening with your body; your whole body listens.

While listening intently in mentoring sessions, I have sometimes experienced a visual impression that a student was moving toward me, even though she was not moving at all. At first I assumed that this meant the student was sharing some particularly important information. Recently I have come to believe that this is a perceptual manifestation of the fact that I am listening deeply and that the student and I are connecting.

Minnich went on to say that there comes a time when the mentor "turns her scanners inward" to see what she has taken in:

> You learn to listen longer with more and more things *open;* you begin to see how much you are always taking in. Before you try to make something out of what you've taken in, you try to describe it to the other person. I often find that when I'm trying to describe or summarize what I've taken in, I can actually lose track of time. Eventually I "come to" and realize that while I was retrieving, I was not tuned in to the outside world at all. It's almost as if I were reading back what I found there and translating it, but keeping the other person and her reaction very much in mind. As I'm describing what I heard, I'm also trying to remain respectful of the person and her reactions.

Analyzing what one has heard occurs in several dimensions. Listening for a student's metaphors, tone, rhythm, and voice has much in common with literary analysis. Watching for how thinking is enacted by the body requires a kind of theatrical analysis. As a philosopher, Minnich said, she also looks for "moves" the student makes.

> I take thinking to be an example of philosophical work which can be analyzed like a philosophical text. My training as a philosopher leads me to speak less about what [the students] say than about what they are *doing.* That is, I try to look for the *moves they make.* I look for basic operating principles—selection, for example. If a student gives a string of examples, I try to hear *through* the selection to the more or less coherent principles which are indications of her inclinations.

Students who have been listened to in this way often describe it as the core of the learning experience. One learner noted:

> The real value of someone listening to your thinking is that it strengthens your own ability to listen. It gives you confidence in your own thinking, even after you've left the educational experience. We've been trained to think that if our thinking is not happening in the prescribed or traditional way, then our thinking is not worthwhile. Part of what I learned was that I *can* think and that I have something to say. My way of thinking was valued. And because it was valued, I can now enter other groups and it no longer matters whether my thinking is valued there. It takes a while to believe that you have a valuable contribution to make—it's something that you have to hear and experience again and again.

In encouraging women to develop their own voices, mentors must be careful to modulate their own. Reentry women are vulnerable to "doing what the teacher wants," a counter-developmental tendency (Taylor, 1991). Yet mentors are far from passive listeners. If mentors are to care for students, they must accept the necessity of challenging learners to think more precisely, more broadly, and more profoundly. They often accomplish this by asking questions.

In traditional educational settings, students frequently come to fear or avoid the teacher's questions; they know that the teacher's intention is either to elicit predetermined answers or to ferret out their ignorance. Far from seeking to catch students in contradictions or label their contributions with jargon or catchwords, mentors try to frame questions that enable learners to reveal their inner intelligence and clarity of thought. One mentor uses open-ended questions such as "Could you tell me more about that?" to invite reentry women to discover their own opinions as they participate in a deeper, more intimate level of conversation. In addition, such questions remind mentors not to step in too quickly with their own answers. As one learner describes it:

> My mentor always asked questions which made me think and which challenged my assumptions. Her questions would knock me off guard in a wonderful way; they helped me make my own decisions and come up with my own answers. She didn't let me get away with anything; she would pick up on those little statements that don't hold a lot of water and question me about them.

Mentors also help students make connections. Traditional, separate knowing is often concerned with making distinctions. Subjects are compartmentalized or atomized; dissociated bits of data must be memorized; learning is structured within disciplines but without a personal context. As the authors of *Women's Ways of Knowing* (Belenky, Clinchy, Goldberger, and Tarule, 1986) point out, even selective liberal arts women's colleges may encourage women's separate procedural knowing at the expense of their developing their own voices. In contrast, the mentor honors making connections as an intellectual activity. The mentor helps the student make connections between apparently contradictory phenomena, between the way the student thought previously and the way she thinks now, between the student's experience and the mentor's knowledge. The mentor builds on the foundation of what the learner already knows, thereby validating and confirming her capacity to know.

Shoulder-to-Shoulder: The Mentor as Companion, Ally, and Sister Learner

Although, as mentioned earlier, there are situations in which a mentor has the experience required to act as a student's guide (particularly insofar as the mentor is well and consciously embarked on her own educational journey), it is the student who must ultimately guide them both toward an as-yet-unknown destination. The mentor listens for and reflects back clues so that the student knows where she is going. In this sense, I think of the mentor as a companion in what Vygotsky calls the "zone of proximal development" (1978).

According to Vygotsky, there is a gap between the level of performance a learner can achieve on her own and the level she can reach with a mentor's support. This gap, the zone of proximal development, represents the student's growing edge; it is the space in which, paradoxically, the learner's grasp exceeds her reach. In traditional educational settings, a student's intelligence and achievement are measured according to what the student can produce alone in an isolated unassisted testing situation. Cooperation or guidance is viewed as cheating. Vygotsky suggests that this approach not only denies the essentially social and interdependent nature of human learning and development, but it results in a flattened, inaccurate underestimation of students' capabilities (1978, p. 80). It also countermands Noddings's insistence (1984) that one function of education is to confirm the student: "When we attribute the highest possible motive consonant with reality to the cared-for, we confirm him; that is, we reveal to him an attainable image of himself that is lovelier than that manifested in his present acts. In an important sense, we embrace him as one with us in devotion to caring. In education, what we reveal to a student about himself as an ethical and intellectual being has the power to nurture the ethical ideal or to destroy it" (p. 193).

The mentor therefore encourages the student to explore the zone of proximal development as fully and freely as possible, for it is here that images of future growth begin to take shape in the student's mind. I have experienced this most frequently while working with students on their writing. There are times at the beginning of the process, for example, when the student dictates while I sit at the computer. Occasionally she will look at her own words with a sense of admiration and surprise and say, "I knew what I was trying to say, but I just couldn't get it down on paper," or even more poignantly, "So *that's* what I've been trying to say all along."

In such cases, the student stands, as Vygotsky puts it, "a head taller than [her]self" (1978, p. 102). She has done something in the presence of her mentor that she could not do alone. Yet she begins to feel a sense of dawning confidence that soon this, too, will be within her independent reach.

As both a mentor and an adult learner, I have observed that many students feel they are chronically or acutely stupid. I have come to believe that one of the mentor's most important roles is to assist in the student's struggle to "undo feeling stupid" and to reclaim her intelligence (Bloom, 1994). For many students, the reclamation of intelligence is a crucial subtext in virtually every learning activity. Mentors can provide direct assistance in this process by helping students demystify, redefine, and enlarge their concept of intelligence (Minnich, 1990, Gardner, 1983); by helping them obtain credit for life experience (Taylor, 1991); by facilitating the design and execution of self-directed learning activities, contracts, and degree programs (Knowles, 1975); and by assisting in what Mezirow (1991) calls "perspective transformation"—in this case, recognizing the extent to which women's feeling stupid helps maintain oppressive control over them in families, schools, and political institutions. The mentor helps the student move from being embedded in a feeling of stupidity to a critical, analytical relationship with that feeling, helping the student see that feeling as a personal, social, and political phenomenon.

Ultimately, caring for the learner by providing a holding environment and by functioning as a guide, a listener, a companion, and an ally becomes a dimension of the mentor's own work as an adult learner and as one learning to care. The mentor remains in place so that, as the student becomes surer of her own educational direction and gains fuller possession of her own voice, the two can meet as sister learners. In order to provide such a model, the mentor must be willing to learn, publicly, alongside the learner. She must be willing to continually explore her own zone of proximal development; develop the capacity to listen, question, and connect; and continuously engage in the reclamation of her own intelligence.

Conclusion

As I think over the many conversations that contributed to the preparation of this chapter, I am struck by mentors' use of words like *luscious, fascinating, delightful, amusing,* and *fun.* What this tells me is that an important (and often overlooked) role of the mentor is to invite the learner to participate in the pleasure of learning—"the erotic" as described by Audre Lorde (1978). Mentors do this, in part, by modeling a healthy relationship to pleasure—intellectual and otherwise. One mentor describes the pleasure of mentoring as follows:

> I feel enormously privileged to be in my office with the sunlight streaming in, with my favorite pictures on the walls and my telephone and books. The students enter in and share bits of themselves with me; and they let me know that I have something they find valuable. I love that people talk to me so intimately— and they can't not talk about themselves when they talk about a book. It's like dancing or a bubble bath. In a humble way, it serves my sense that there is kindness in the world.

Not only are mentors able to enjoy the diverse ways of thinking their students exhibit, but even when they disagree with or are disappointed by their students' work, mentors enjoy their own engagement with and processing of that work. When I commented on this to another mentor, she pointed out a still broader dimension of the mentor's pleasure:

> Part of my mentor's commitment to clear thinking is in the service of social change and social justice, as a means toward a more ethical way of being. I remember learning about Hannah Arendt's comment that Nazism was possible, in part, because people didn't think. In our culture, thinking is a challenge because society is telling us in many different ways not to think and to let others do our thinking for us. Helping people think is part of the mentor's ethical commitment; there is pleasure in seeing that happen.

References

Belenky, M. F., Clinchy, B. M., Goldberger, N. R., and Tarule, J. M. *Women's Ways of Knowing: The Development of Self, Voice, and Mind.* New York: Basic Books, 1986.

Bloom, M. "The Reclamation of Intelligence: A Task for Adult Learners." Unpublished doctoral dissertation, Union Graduate School, The Union Institute, 1994.

Daloz, L. A. *Effective Teaching and Mentoring: Realizing the Transformational Power of Adult Learning Experiences.* San Francisco: Jossey-Bass, 1986.

Gardner, H. *Frames of Mind: The Theory of Multiple Intelligences.* New York: Basic Books, 1983.

Gilligan, C. *In a Different Voice: Psychological Theory and Women's Development.* Cambridge, Mass.: Harvard University Press, 1982.

Kegan, R. *The Evolving Self: Problem and Process in Human Development.* Cambridge, Mass.: Harvard University Press, 1982.

Kegan, R. *In Over Our Heads: The Mental Demands of Modern Life.* Cambridge, Mass.: Harvard University Press, 1994.

Knowles, M. S. *Self-Directed Learning: A Guide for Learners and Teachers.* New York: Association Press, 1975.

Lorde, A. "The Uses of the Erotic: The Erotic as Power." *Sister Outsider: Essays and Speeches.* Freedom, Calif.: Crossing Press, 1978.

McIntosh, P. "Feeling Like a Fraud." Stone Center Working Papers Series, Works in Progress, No. 18. Wellesley, Mass.: Stone Center for Developmental Services and Studies, 1985.

Mezirow, J. *Transformative Dimensions of Adult Learning.* San Francisco: Jossey-Bass, 1991.

Minnich, E. K. *Transforming Knowledge.* Philadelphia: Temple University Press, 1990.

Noddings, N. *Caring: A Feminine Approach to Ethics and Moral Education.* Berkeley: University of California Press, 1984.

Taylor, K. "Transforming Learning: Experiences of Adult Development and Transformation of Re-entry Learners in an Adult Degree Program." Unpublished doctoral dissertation, Union Graduate School, The Union Institute, 1991.

Taylor, K. "Teaching to Support Women's Adult Development." *Thought & Action,* 1994, *10* (1), 57–72.

Vygotsky, L. *Mind in Society: The Development of Higher Psychological Processes.* Cambridge, Mass.: Harvard University Press, 1978.

MAYRA BLOOM is a mentor at Empire State College, State University of New York, where she works with adult learners in individualized undergraduate degree programs in educational studies, developmental psychology, and writing.

Learning-centered teaching strategies that support women's development are based on connections among ideas about learning, teaching, and development.

Linking Learning, Teaching, and Development

Morris Fiddler, Catherine Marienau

> To teach is to participate in the conversation that is learning. The moment we move away from the table around which conversation is created—where meanings are re-created, where imagination and reason are bridged—we move a step away from the dynamic of living. Being a part of each other's development—in the re-defining of the self, in the change and exchange of new knowledge—is engaging each other, we and students, in the affirmation and wonder of living, in the conversation at the table, in development.
> —Morris Fiddler and Catherine Marienau, in conversation, 1994

Our insights into teaching, learning, and development, and their interconnections, have been greatly enhanced by our free-flowing conversations over the years and more intense conversations during the months of preparing this chapter. At the heart of our conversations are lessons learned from what our students say has been important to them.

> She made the difficult easy and fun to digest and now I offer people information differently; I exchange information differently with people—in my relationships, with my parents, with my friends. . . . And I read different things now and turn them back on myself with a new sense of respect for my experience. . . . I finally understand that my achievements were impressive on their own, with or without approval. I actually read more things now that make me uncomfortable . . . and I don't see authors as gospel anymore . . . we talk to each other. . . which has made learning more a part of my growing. [An undergraduate woman learner, 1993]

It was a math teacher from whom I learned how to sort out the "noise" from the hearts of the matters in my life. She listened to some stories of me when I was having trouble with the class and found analogies to the concepts of trigonometry; she actually helped me to see connections to what I already knew to map the stories onto new stuff. I do this all the time now, like a transparency overlaid to give me a map of my problems—in my relationships, in my work, in my changes. The themes become metaphors, and the metaphors help me to categorize and sort things out; I've carried this long past math. [An undergraduate woman learner, 1993]

The themes of conversation and connection—with others, with oneself, with course material—are embedded in these remarks from two women returning to college. Both women display evidence of development as described in the literature—an increased reliance on internal criteria, effective strategies to respond to life events, and a heightened sense of self-awareness and competence. These women's reflections on their experiences suggest that individual development can be prompted by a good teacher and a good course. We speculate that individual development can be supported by different teaching aims, from the more limited aim of transmitting knowledge to the more expansive and explicit aim of individual, or even social, transformation.

What was it, then, about the particular courses and teachers these women encountered that stimulated their development? We can infer from what we actually know about these women, about the courses, and about their teachers that the teachers placed an accent on learning, making it the central issue. They drew on learners' experience, engaging them in reflective conversation with their experience as well as with each other and the material. As a result, these women gained and later drew on learning strategies that they continued to use beyond these initial interactions.

By listening to these women and other learners, reflecting on our experiences, examining theories and models, and exploring our intuitions, we have come to recognize that teaching is most powerful when it focuses on learning—in both cognitive and affective realms—and when it is informed by an understanding both of the continuously developing adult and of learning per se. This approach to teaching is what ultimately links learning to development. We assume, and our experience bears this out, that both women and men are well served through learning-centered teaching.

Teaching as a Link Between Learning and Development

Educators are fortunate today in that a discussion of teaching and development can now take advantage of a wealth of experience and theory in adult learning and development (particularly women's development) and feminist pedagogy. Figure 9.1 illustrates our emerging conception of learning-centered teaching as a link between learning and development. One enters the image through the center—the premises of learning. Although all people learn differently, learning is in essence an iterative, interactive, purposeful, and unpredictable process. These premises inform teaching that is learning-centered, the distinguishing characteristics of which are presented on the left-hand side of the figure. The synergy of teaching, informed by characteristics of learning itself, supports women's development as a lifelong process that involves a variety of cognitive and affective dimensions, represented on the right-hand side of the figure.

We advance the proposition that teaching that best supports development offers a learner models for managing learning—inside and outside the academic context, in a variety of independent and social settings, and in relationship with a variety of others and a myriad of subjects. Ideally the models will be rich and varied enough to accommodate the wide-ranging differences among women learners as well as their commonalities.

Different Lives, Common Themes: Experience as the Common Denominator

Figure 9.1 illustrates strikingly common themes concerning learning and women's development—themes that cut across various models of adult development, whether stage, phase, or cyclical. These commonalities are striking because the more we listen to and get to know our students, the more we are reminded that there is less similarity within a group of sixty-, forty-, or thirty-year-olds than within a group of six-year-olds (Neugarten, 1979). Yet, while students' lives are indeed growing different from each other's, we see common themes in the concepts of acceptance, responsibility, and self-definition (Peck, 1986). We see the rhythm of fluidity and discontinuity (Caffarella and Olson, 1993). We see reassessment of meaning serving as a driver of one's future (Carlsen, 1988), and we see transformation of perspectives (Tennant, 1993).

The notion that women grow more different from one another as they get older but that they nonetheless have much in common developmentally across an adult life span presents a challenging paradox for teachers. We suggest that focusing on learners' experience can help teachers negotiate this paradox in meaningful ways. Personal experience has become a legitimate arena of intellectual inquiry (Dewey, 1938; Kolb, 1984; Culley and Portuges, 1985; Belenky, Clinchy, Goldberger, and Tarule, 1986). Furthermore, as Maher (1985) and Maher and Tetreault (1994) point out, one of the assumptions of the emerging scholarship on women is that appropriate teaching styles to recover the female experience can also be applied to the education of all people. Personal experience serves as a critical source of motivation, learning, and meaning making to help the developing woman heighten awareness of her self; recognize shifts in her life; identify needs, dilemmas, or challenges that may require social action or new adaptive strategies; and carry on an invested dialogue with others about ideas, topics, and experiences.

Figure 9.1. Learning-Centered Teaching:
A Path Between Learning and Development

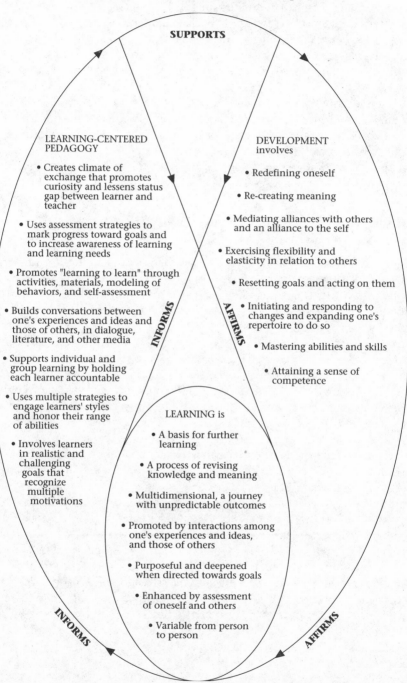

SUPPORTS

LEARNING-CENTERED
PEDAGOGY

- Creates climate of
  exchange that promotes
  curiosity and lessens status
  gap between learner and
  teacher

- Uses assessment strategies to
  mark progress toward goals and
  to increase awareness of learning
  and learning needs

- Promotes "learning to learn" through
  activities, materials, modeling of
  behaviors, and self-assessment

- Builds conversations between
  one's experiences and ideas and
  those of others, in dialogue,
  literature, and other media

- Supports individual and
  group learning by holding
  each learner accountable

- Uses multiple strategies to
  engage learners' styles
  and honor their range
  of abilities

- Involves learners
  in realistic and
  challenging
  goals that
  recognize
  multiple
  motivations

DEVELOPMENT
involves

- Redefining oneself

- Re-creating meaning

- Mediating alliances with others
  and an alliance to the self

- Exercising flexibility and
  elasticity in relation to others

- Resetting goals and acting on them

- Initiating and responding to
  changes and expanding one's
  repertoire to do so

- Mastering abilities and skills

- Attaining a sense of
  competence

INFORMS   AFFIRMS

LEARNING is

- A basis for further
  learning

- A process of revising
  knowledge and meaning

- Multidimensional, a journey
  with unpredictable outcomes

- Promoted by interactions among
  one's experiences and ideas,
  and those of others

- Purposeful and deepened
  when directed towards goals

- Enhanced by assessment
  of oneself and others

- Variable from person
  to person

INFORMS   AFFIRMS

I've been at this [thesis] for two months and I know I've got a good outline and information—but I just [got] stuck . . . until a couple of days ago, when your question, "Why do you care about health and health care?" kept haunting me. And I finally realized that [in] the three major encounters my family and I have had with physicians and the "system"—they failed us each time. . . . Now I can get into the dialogue with what I've been reading, knowing what it is I'm looking to understand. . . . I've been defining my professional work without exactly knowing why it's mine. [An undergraduate woman learner, 1993]

As this woman learner points out, the key to her ownership of her life direction, at least professionally, is in her experience, in her reflection on and understanding of that experience, and in her use of it to make meaning of her current efforts. Kegan (1982) observed that the most fundamental thing we do with what happens to us is to organize it—we *make* sense; our being and becoming is rooted in the composing of meaning. Learning, then, is not just about behavioral change, but also about the complexities of meaning formation (Clark, 1993), which is both the outcome and essence of learning. Our students have similarly told us that "we learn to make sense of the world" (Fiddler, 1994). Implicit in our image is the overarching belief that the experiences of reentering women reflect activities and processes that cut across a variety of developmental models.

Teaching Strategies in Support of Development

The dynamics of adult development and the strategies of learning-centered pedagogy correspond in consequential ways. We want to note that we are dealing at the conceptual level of learning strategy—with approaches to engaging learners with the material and with each other rather than with technique or specific how-to's. Teaching strategies that support development meet at least these criteria: they are transferable to the learner (in other words, the learner can use them in various settings), congruent with gender-related learning modes, and geared to characteristics of the developing adult.

An analogy between learning and music composition may help to illuminate our view of learning-centered teaching strategies. Learning is often an exploration of a limited set of ideas, like themes or motifs in music, that are analyzed for their elements (rhythms, harmonies, notes) and then explored, altered, and elaborated on by application of various techniques or conventions. If one is good, one's learning can be insightful and meaningful, just as one's composing can be artful. And just as a composer begins with a theme or motif, learning-centered teaching helps learners identify and concentrate on significant ideas and themes in both cognitive and affective domains. Learning-centered teaching includes a variety of strategies that incorporate techniques to help the learner elaborate on those themes or ideas. There is, of course, no formulaic approach to this process—each decision is an aesthetic judgment. Ideas are dictated by content and techniques are dictated by strategy.

Strategies of learning-centered teaching should also be seen in the context of larger considerations of teaching per se. We find it helpful to set strategies within the additional context of models that rest on the relationships among the learner, the teacher, and the content. These models, suggested by Pratt (1992), are drawn from and cut across multiple cultures. They provide a framework for describing the range of approaches to teaching that teachers move among, often without conscious or deliberate shifts. The five configurations of these models include engineering, apprenticeship, developmental (cognitive), nurturing, and social reform. Though several of these terms have meanings in other contexts, Pratt uses them to describe the conceptual relationships among the teacher, the learner, and the content, not the teaching of any particular subject (such as engineering).

We extend these conceptions of teaching by presenting in Table 9.1 some strategies that are compatible with the primary elements (for example, teacher-content, learner-content) of each model and that are particularly consistent with the joint dynamics of learning-centered pedagogy, women's and adult development, and transferability to the learner. For example, the engineering model of teaching emphasizes the elements of teaching and content and the teacher's concern for and authority over that which is to be learned. Strategies consistent with the criteria for teaching for development for this model could include the presentation of information through metaphors and encouragement of students to reorganize content through metaphors of their own. One of the women we quoted at the beginning of this chapter provides support for this suggestion. Similarly, self-assessment (see Chapter Three) may serve as an effective strategy for three of the models: developmental (cognitive), nurturing, and social reform.

While we may lean toward one or two of these teaching models as our primary choices to facilitate adult learning (the developmental and nurturing models for example), each of the five models can serve well to deliver curriculum in varying circumstances. However, the choice of strategies can enhance or promote development as we have been describing it and relating it to teaching and learning throughout this chapter.

As flexible and reflective practitioners (see Schön, 1981) and as teachers, we aim to move freely and intentionally among the relationships described by Pratt, just as we would want to move among multiple positions in any conversation. Movement among these relationships may be facilitated through the approaches or strategies teachers adopt in practice. The grace of that movement is related, in part, to how clearly the teaching strategies inform a general conception of teaching integrated with the linkage of learning, learning-centered pedagogy, and development. A few brief quotes from adult learners offer some affirmation of several teaching strategies indicated in Table 9.1 and consonant with links between learning and development. These learners appear to have added to their repertoires learning strategies that can serve them in ongoing processes of adapting to changes that mark development.

Table 9.1. Conceptions of Teaching and Related Teaching Strategies

Model	Primary Elements	Some Teaching Strategies
Engineering	Teacher and content; teacher's concern for and authority over that to be learned	Presenting information through metaphors and analogies Encouraging students to reorganize content through metaphors of their own
Apprenticeship	Teacher and content; teacher and content "inseparable"; teacher exemplifies values and knowledge to be learned	Behavior modeling Mutual assessment (teacher and student)
Developmental (Cognitive)	Learners and teacher; inquiry and thought about content to promote cognitive development	Self-assessment Peer assessment Collaborative inquiry and individual accountability Relating and redefining connections among ideas (theories) and experiences Problem-centered exercises
Nurturing	Learner and teacher; focus on learner's self-concept and personal agency; learning facilitated by mutual trust, reciprocal respect	Responsive course design Self-assessment Dialogue Appreciation of a range of perspectives, knowledge, and abilities
Social Reform	Explicit ideal or principles linked to vision of improved social order; emphasis on social, cultural, and political elements or on imperatives that override elements of teacher-learner-content	Modeling expression of ideal and behaviors Dialogue Self-assessment

Source: First and second columns adapted from Pratt, 1992.

Well, it really wasn't about jazz. It was about taking risks and dialogue and a few other ideas about living (in this class about writing!). [Model: engineering. Strategy: presenting information through metaphor.]

I have found uses for problem-based learning in my family problems as well as organizational work. . . . It's more like the way I think outside of school. [Model: developmental. Strategy: problem-centered exercises.]

Through a more conscious look at my life's activities I have developed a new sense of my purpose and a clearer vision of my (professional) goals. [Model: nurturing. Strategy: self-assessment.]

Development as an Aim of Education: Some Ethical Concerns

As we reflect on conceptions of teaching in support of development and on strategies that may promote development, we affirm a belief that development through the teaching-learning nexus is both desirable and possible as an aim of education. We also recognize that adult development is an evolving process, without prescribed or predictable ends. As teachers, all of us can provide a place for each person around the table of conversation, for the engagement of each person in the experience of her own development, for the exercise of learner freedom and human agency. While the tenets of andragogy rest on these qualities of freedom and agency, these tenets are not universal in adult education (Pratt, 1993).

The aims of formal education vary among institutions, programs, teachers, and learners; they fall along a continuum that includes the transmission of knowledge, the demonstration of competency, the expansion of cognitive acumen, holistic development, and social action—often in some combination. Developmental outcomes for women reentering education are often viewed in some quarters, therefore, as "value-added" and not common or central to standards of practice in the academy. Though we can, *should* we provide a place for each person to engage in the experience of her own development? The extent to which it is appropriate to enter the lives of our students beyond the formalities of the curriculum is not always clear.

The diversity of educational aims frames the lack of widely accepted ethical constructs within which to discuss and make judgments regarding expectations and limitations of our roles, obligations, privileges, and responsibilities as teachers. This is particularly challenging as we further our understanding and recognition that the women (and men) with whom we work bring to the formal educational setting a myriad of developmental, experiential, cultural, and other dimensions that influence their motivations and purposes for seeking and making meaning of new learning. Any conversation about our practice may do well to seek guidance from applied ethics. Perhaps, through a description and examination of the choices we encounter, we can sort ethical questions from those of standards of practice and assess the value of various approaches—for example, categorical, as in medicine (Beauchamp and Childress, 1983), and relational (Fletcher, 1989; Lyons, 1988)—that lead to appropriate and practical judgments as we respond to our students.

These considerations notwithstanding, the adoption of strategies that may support development offers us all, as teachers-learners and learners-teachers, avenues to manage our learning, to expand our capacities to develop, to change social realities, to contribute to the development of others in our lives, and to adapt and evolve as an active affirmation "of the unique dimensions of age and aging" (Friedan, 1993).

> I've gotten a little from many teachers, [from] some a good deal more. One of the ways I know that is by recognizing the "how" I learn in what I learn. . . . Only one teacher ever expected me to change, and I wasn't comfortable with that . . . but several others left me with things I've used and passed on to others, too. [Adult learner]

References

Beauchamp, T. L., and Childress, J. F. *Principles of Biomedical Ethics.* (2nd ed.) New York: Oxford University Press, 1983.

Belenky, M. F., Clinchy, B. M., Goldberger, N. R., and Tarule, J. M. *Women's Ways of Knowing: The Development of Self, Voice, and Mind.* New York: Basic Books, 1986.

Caffarella, R., and Olson, S. "Psychosocial Development of Women: A Critical Review of the Literature." *Adult Education Quarterly,* 1993, 43 (1), 125–151.

Carlsen, M. B. *Meaning Making.* New York: Norton, 1988.

Clark, M. C. "Transformational Learning." In S. B. Merriam (ed.), *An Update on Adult Learning Theory.* New Directions for Adult and Continuing Education, no. 57. San Francisco: Jossey-Bass, 1993.

Culley, M., and Portuges, C. Introduction to M. Culley and C. Portuges (eds.), *Gendered Subjects: The Dynamics of Feminist Teaching.* New York: Routledge & Kegan Paul, 1985.

Dewey, J. *Experience and Education.* New York: Collier, 1938.

Fiddler, M. B. "Teaching to Competence: Enhancing the Art of Teaching (Adults)." *Journal of General Education,* 1994, 43, 289–303.

Fletcher, J. C. "Ethics and Human Genetics: A Cross-Cultural Perspective." In D. C. Wertz and J. C. Fletcher (eds.), *Ethics and Human Genetics.* New York: Springer-Verlag, 1989.

Friedan, B. *The Fountain of Age.* New York: Simon & Schuster, 1993.

Kegan, R. *The Evolving Self: Problem and Process in Human Development.* Cambridge, Mass.: Harvard University Press, 1982.

Kolb, D. *Experiential Learning: Experience as the Source of Learning and Development.* Englewood Cliffs, N.J.: Prentice Hall, 1984.

Lyons, N. P. "Two Perspectives: On Self, Relationships, and Morality." In C. Gilligan, J. V. Ward, and J. M. Taylor (eds.), *Mapping the Moral Domain.* Cambridge, Mass.: Harvard University Press, 1988.

Maher, F. "Classroom Pedagogy and the New Scholarship on Women." In M. Culley and C. Portuges (eds.), *Gendered Subjects: The Dynamics of Feminist Teaching.* New York: Routledge & Kegan Paul, 1985.

Maher, F. A., and Tetreault, M. K. *The Feminist Classroom: An Inside Look at How Professors and Students Are Transforming Higher Education in a Diverse Society.* New York: Basic Books, 1994.

Neugarten, B. "Time, Age, and the Life Cycle." *American Journal of Psychiatry*, 1979, *136* (7), 887–894.

Peck, T. "Women's Self-Definition in Adulthood: From a Different Model?" *Psychology of Women Quarterly*, 1986, *10*, 274–284.

Pratt, D. "Conceptions of Teaching." *Adult Education Quarterly*, 1992, *42*, 203–220.

Pratt, D. "Andragogy After Twenty-Five Years." In S. B. Merriam (ed.), *An Update on Adult Learning Theory*. New Directions for Adult and Continuing Education, no. 57. San Francisco: Jossey-Bass, 1993.

Schön, D. *The Reflective Practitioner*. New York: Basic Books, 1981.

Tennant, M. "Perspective Transformation and Adult Development." *Adult Education Quarterly*, 1993, *44*, 34–42.

MORRIS FIDDLER is a senior fellow at the School for New Learning at DePaul University. He has been working with and learning from adult learners in a variety of contexts for about twenty years.

CATHERINE MARIENAU is associate professor in the School for New Learning at DePaul University and is active in the Alliance (an association for alternative degree programs for adults).

Women whose educational experiences resulted in change describe the learning environments that support development of self-authored and self-authorizing identity.

Speaking Her Mind: Adult Learning and Women's Adult Development

Kathleen Taylor

Who is the reentry woman as she moves through and reflects on her educational experience? Again and again, we hear her speak of changing in important ways: *I am not who I was.*

Alix, thirty-five at reentry, is Caucasian and single.

> I can stand my ground. I have effectively faced a self-debilitating pattern of thinking that was limiting how I functioned in the world and my relationship with myself and others. . . . I am a different person.

Betty, sixty-two at reentry, is Caucasian and married.

> Everybody [in my family] has had to change. . . . I was the one that recognized it and said, "Hey, [*laughter*] this is not going to work for me [anymore]. . . . Then [my husband and children] realized it's not ever going to be like it was [before school] . . . easy for everybody to depend on [me]. . . . [Now] I have my life too.

Charlotte, thirty-eight at reentry, is Caucasian and divorced.

> For some reason, I had to look at my essay for admission again and . . . I read it and I thought about the person who wrote it being so almost apologetic for who she was at that time—and [I thought] to myself, "I don't have to apologize for who I am anymore."

Jackie, thirty-five at reentry, is African American and divorced.

I've just changed completely from when I first [reentered school]. I used to take this little African body and force it into this European square peg. And you know, it didn't work. I kept trying to do it and trying to change who I was and tried to fit in. . . . When I finally decided to be the person that I am, I started feeling more comfortable.

Janet, thirty-four at reentry, is Caucasian and divorced.

[I've moved] from one way of experiencing the world to a very different one—tolerating the awareness that I am ultimately responsible for myself. . . . I may have been given all these—it's kind of like that quilt maker—you get all these pieces in life and those are the ones you get. And what you can afford you get, and what you're given is what you get. But it's how you put it together that makes the difference—that emphasis on how I put it together, not on what I get.

In this chapter, we will attend closely to the voices of women who identified change or growth as an outcome of their educational experiences (Taylor, 1991). Using Kegan's model as a framework, we will explore the implications of these changes for the women themselves, their families and communities, and the greater society; we will also examine the role education played in their transformation.

Kegan's Model of Development

Why do so many reentry women report being a different person than who they once were? How is coming back to school linked with reconstructing their identities? I have found that Kegan's constructive-developmental model (1982, 1994) best illuminates these women's experiences of who they were and who they have become, specifically in terms of the move from third- to fourth-order consciousness (or the 3 → 4 shift, using his earlier terminology). But before we can examine the specifics, we must examine the basis of the theory. Constructivists hold that how we make meaning—how we perceive the world and ourselves—creates reality as we know it. As Kegan explains it, "[there is] no feeling, no experience, no thought, no perception, independent of a meaning-making context in which it *becomes* a feeling, an experience, a thought, a perception, because we *are* the meaning-making context" (1982, p. 11). Kegan's theory of development describes a series of qualitative changes in that meaning-making context—that is, in ourselves—each of which, in turn, changes the meanings we make. (See Chapters One and Three for further discussion of Kegan's model.)

An organizing principle of the third order of consciousness, which Kegan initially called the "interpersonal" stage of development, is mutuality. This is not just garden-variety reciprocity or empathy. This is a construction within which a person thinks, believes, and acts on the premise that she "just is" a certain way; furthermore, she cannot control many of her responses to the needs and feelings of others. For example, she can be "made" to feel certain ways ("Why do you always make me feel so guilty when I [fill in the blank]?"). Similarly, she takes responsibility for how others feel ("I got them so mad at me"). Also, "others" is a rather sizeable category. It extends beyond immediate or distant family members, co-workers, or any particular identifiable community; a woman at the third order of consciousness experiences herself as responsible for and affected by everything and everyone in what Kegan calls the "psychological surround." This is not something she chooses, nor is she even aware of it in the way just described. As with every order of consciousness, to the person embedded or enmeshed in it, its organizing principle is invisible—and totally pervasive. She "can't help" seeing the world or feeling the way she does. Moreover, rather than emanating from her and being her construction of herself, her identity is reflected onto her, constructed from all the "identities" that others create for her: "I seem to believe there is no Me except in other eyes. I am what I see in your eyes, whoever you are" (Koller, 1983, p. 94).

By contrast, an organizing principle of the fourth order of consciousness, which Kegan initially called the "institutional" stage of development, is perspective on her (and others') reactions, beliefs, experiences, values, and relationships—these things are no longer "just the way I am" (or "the way things are" or "the way people are"). She can look at her former reality and see its contradictions and limitations (of course, she cannot see the contradictions and limitations of her current order of consciousness). She not only comes to recognize that her feelings, for example, are hers, that they are not "caused" by someone else, but she can also examine and explore them, articulate her ownership of them, and even, if not totally control them, at least recognize them as products of her interpretation and perception. She also realizes that she does not "cause" anyone else's feelings. At home, in her community, and at work, she can separate her loyalty to and feelings for friends, co-workers, or loved ones from her beliefs, values, or actions with which they may not agree. For example, Kegan (1982) reports the comments of a woman speaking from the perspective of fourth-order consciousness, describing her former self.

> I wasn't always this way. I used to have two sets of clothes—one for my husband and one for my mother who visited often. Two sets of clothes, but none for me. Now I dress in my clothes. Some of them are like what my mother would like me to wear but that's a totally different thing [p. 241].

We hear most often about changes in reentry women's familial or affectional relationships. One woman, Jackie, observed that:

> Male-female relationships [have] always been one of my weak points. . . . I could spot a man with "potential" ten miles away. "Ah, he's got potential and I can change that man." I finally learned that people have to be who they are. . . . And I'm dealing with it from a whole different perspective than [ever before]. . . . [What] I would have done before was like: "OK, maybe if I were thinner, or if I

looked like this, or [wore] my hair like that, maybe then." But now, this is who I am and . . . I don't feel the need to put down who I am, and a lot of times . . . I tore myself down in order to make them feel comfortable.

Indeed, Jackie does have a "whole different perspective." In moving toward fourth-order consciousness, she has discovered (constructed) her own self: a self to which she can have a clearer allegiance than the one that was constructed in response to others' constructions of her. Note the difference between the power of the fourth order's self-appraisal ("This is who I am [subtext: I love it]") and the third order's apologetic tone ("This is *just* who I am [subtext: I can't help it]").

A reader of Kegan's first representation of this model (1982) could have inferred that, especially for women, the interpersonal stage (the third order) was all about having relationships and that developing to the institutional (the fourth order) implied somehow growing beyond relationships. He has since changed and clarified his model to make explicit that *each* stage of development or order of consciousness finds expression in *both* of the "two greatest yearnings of human life . . . to be welcomed in, next to, held, connected with, a part of . . . [and] to be autonomous, independent, to experience my own agency, the self-chosenness of my purpose" (1982, p. 142). Gilligan (1982) suggests that women fundamentally tend more often than men toward relatedness, connection, and the ethic of caring (whereas men tend more often than women toward independence, separation, and the ethic of justice); Tavris (1992) holds that this is a "mismeasure" of women. Whether or not this is so, until recently women's primary roles have revolved around relatedness and connection; thus development for women has involved what appeared to be a pathological choice, between a self-authored identity and loving relationships.

But the transition to fourth-order consciousness does not require that connections be severed, only transformed. In an earlier study, I wrote that "despite their new-found abilities to establish boundaries, these women do not appear to have lost [their] fundamental orientation toward connection; what has changed is their relationship to it. Burdette [described in Chapters One and Three] for example, still emphasizes her family responsibilities; but she no longer disappears into that role. Jackie [described in this chapter] definitely wants to find a successful relationship with a man; but not if it means she has to pretend to be other than who she is. Betty [described in this chapter and Chapter One] will never go back to being the way she was [everyone's caretaker]; but her daughters' development is still a major concern for her" (Taylor, 1991, p. 90). Nevertheless, if a spousal relationship has been built on "affiliation, nurturance, and identification," it may not stand the shift to "distinctness, independence, or cooperation of separate interests" (Kegan, 1982, p. 219), hence the near-cliché about reentry women getting a degree for a divorce.

The consequences of the shift to fourth-order consciousness reach beyond a woman's primary relationships, however. In her workplace, she will come to see the difference between the way her job is structured and the way she structures her job. Because she can look *at* the organization she works for, and not merely take on its perspective, she is more likely than her third-order-consciousness co-workers to contribute effectively to many of the new managerial approaches such as TQM (Total Quality Management), quality circles, and bottom-up or flattened-out organizational structures. (Of course, if the organization is run on third-order principles—a top-down hierarchy, a "just do your job" mentality—her shift to fourth-order consciousness can lead to an increasingly poor fit.) The literature on leadership suggests that a woman at the fourth order of consciousness may become an "empowered" and "empowering" manager (Caffarella, 1992).

In her interactions with the wider community, she will recognize that her way (and her group's way—whether that group is based on, for example, ideology, culture, race, religion, or political party) is not the *right* way, it is *a* way; that, as Kegan points out, it is a style or a preference and not the result of superior apprehension. If she is in psychotherapy, she will be able to use insight as a bridge to change, rather than just discovering why she is the way she is. She will begin to take responsibility for her interactions and her feelings; she will reconstruct her beliefs in light of a value system *she* creates—one she recognizes as her creation and maintains a continuing dialogue with—rather than her former value system, which emanated from the psychological surround and could not be questioned.

The Role of Education in Transformation

Some of the women who return to college have probably already begun the shift from third- to fourth-order consciousness. They often articulate their desire for a new, self-authored identity. As one student put it, "I knew I had to do something with my life, that I could no longer . . . just be wife and mother and daughter and sister." Others may not consciously realize that coming back to school is part of a process of transition. But in either case, their transformation is likely to affect and be affected by their academic experiences.

The Need for Support. Paradoxically, women engaged in growth toward fourth-order consciousness sometimes resist the very development toward self-authorization that they seek. This may be due partly to a lack of confidence, especially about things academic. They return to school anxious but determined, believing that success lies in "doing what the teacher wants." This can be counter-developmental behavior. When educators unwittingly collude by joining the voices in the psychological surround rather than inviting a woman to begin to hear and speak in her own voice, these women merely add "student" to the roles that others have defined for them. In contrast, learning-centered teaching strategies (described in Chapter Nine) recognize the individual learner, thereby encouraging development of the individual.

Some women's reluctance may also stem from a fear of losing the self they know or the relationships they are comfortable with. Daloz's cautionary tale (1988) about "Gladys who refused to grow" reminds us that the desire for development must come from the learner herself. Sometimes, however, she is just temporarily overwhelmed, and active support can make a difference.

> I came in . . . to express that it really and truly didn't matter anymore to me. That it was more than I could deal with. . . . And you came back at me that you didn't [perceive] it that way and that I was psychologically setting myself up for failure and it was the "fear of success" kind of syndrome. And I'm not sure if that was valid—I'm not sure [whether] it made me so angry that I felt you weren't perceiving that what I said was valid and true for me, and that I'd definitely [*laughter*] have to kill myself to prove it, or if that was exactly the prod that I needed. . . . [I did feel] a real genuineness from you [to] . . . recognize and appreciate my strength and talent and wanting to help me get the stuff together. So I think that was real magical that that happened.

The returning learner needs acknowledgement of her skills and support to overcome her weaknesses. She needs to be deeply seen and heard, and she needs to be recognized, as Janet said, "as an individual with some of my own quirks." Jackie also observed:

> You know we all look for validation. We say we don't but we all do. When you're young you get it from your parents all the time, but you think, "Well, [they're] my parents, they're my family, they gotta say that kind of stuff." [It means more] when you get it from the outside world—"It's OK you did this. It's OK what you did." [Getting] that [in this program] was real important to me.

Paradoxically, if she gets this validation when she needs it, the reentry woman may soon outgrow the need. Alix discovered:

> I was looking [in the beginning] for external reinforcement constantly. . . . [But] I got the amount of feedback and reinforcement that I needed, until I started to know what the response was going to be. Then I wasn't as anxious to . . . find out "Was this OK?"

In Chapter Eight, Mayra Bloom describes the position of the mentor in the reentry woman's journey: in front of her, to guide her; behind her, to encourage her; face-to-face with her, to mirror her; and beside her, as the mentor undertakes her own journey. Other chapters in this sourcebook, though not specifically about mentoring, describe similar supports for the journey of development.

Most programs are not structured explicitly around mentoring relationships; however, the reentry woman needs *someone* to care, to pay attention, to listen, to nurture—the personal and familial supports she has available are often lukewarm (Marienau, 1976). In fact, the people closest to her may feel so threatened by the possibility of change that they kick supports out from under her. This happened to Penny, who dropped out in her third quarter and never returned:

"You think you're better than us," was coming from my mother at one point [*nervous laugh*] . . . "High and mighty" [*nervous laugh*]. . . . I was trying to work full time, still be the Room Mother, and still drive the kids to school, and be there on time, and feed the dog, and make sure that dinner was on the table at five o'clock. . . . The kids called me by my first name, I remember that. That was a big joke in the house. . . . Because they said they didn't see me anymore. . . . There was a lot of complaining that there had to be baby-sitting done and I wasn't earning money at it—at what I was making him baby-sit for.

Given a woman's traditional roles as nurturer and caregiver, the reentry woman is unlikely to ask for the support she may desperately need. She may not even know it is a need, or if she does, she often feels undeserving, at some level, of another's (especially an authority figure's) invested regard. One effective programmatic approach is to build peer support, collaborative learning, or cohort groups into the program. Reentry women are too busy, and may be too insecure, to reach out to others on their own—especially during the early period just after reentry, when it is most crucial.

The Need for Self-Direction. Candy (1991) describes a confusion between means and ends in the literature on self-direction—a confusion between the *process* of self-direction in learning (being asked or required to take greater responsibility) and that process's *product,* a learner capable of self-direction. However, reentry learners experience the two as intertwined. As they speak about their new sense of self, a self that has grown beyond the boundaries of being "a good student" and now feels responsible and empowered in relationship to learning, reentry women describe the requirement for self-direction as among the most valuable and change-inducing aspects of their reentry experiences. For example, when Janet had to construct her own learning plans, she found that:

[There's] not as much of the role, "I'm going to do this for [my advisor]." [She's] there, but I'm doing this for me. So, having that shift [to construct one's own course outline] be there makes my thinking better altogether. It reinforces: be responsible for yourself. How are you going to do this whole thing? How are you going to make your [plan] meaningful? How are you going to make this class meaningful? When are you going to get this work done? Are you going to do it at the end of the quarter again? How much are you really going to learn; how much do you want to learn? Always these questions, questions, questions all the time. . . . I never asked this before. It's really heightened my awareness of "How are you going to function in this life?"

Kathy described how the research she had to do in order to set up her learning plan changed her perception of what she was capable of.

[My instructor] suggested a book, but he said "find other things to read. There's a lot out there . . . think of what else you could do to learn more about [the subject]." So *that,* that can only lead to growth. . . . [I found out] I only have to be pointed in the right direction and that I can be resourceful.

Barbara found that self-directed learning brought back her love of learning.

Doing it pretty much on my own . . . was so exciting to me. It reminded me . . . [of] sitting there as a child thinking about it, thinking: "Oh, my brain!" I would *experience* it—taking in information. And I *loved* that experience. And that's what started happening again. I didn't think I'd ever have it again. . . . [It resulted from] just the doing it, just taking [the instructor's] advice, just taking these books home and doing it, not expecting somebody else to teach it to me. Just grappling with it . . . and hang[ing] in until I got it. That was just fun. It made me feel confident. [In other college experiences] someone else gave it to me. They had done all the thinking. I didn't have to learn to think; I could memo-rize. . . . I certainly didn't practice thinking, thinking through a problem.

It is crucial, of course, to meet the learner where she is along the contin-uum of self-direction. (This is the guiding principle behind Ursuline College's curriculum revision described in Chapter Seven.) Not everyone has Barbara's capacity—and desire—to go off and do it largely on her own. Charlotte felt "at first, I was lost." Alix had to "struggle." Another student was

A little unnerv[ed], a little frighten[ed] because all of these things were being suggested for the first time. . . . The fact that you *do* direct your own course. That nobody's going to stand there and tell you exactly what steps to take. . . . I think along the way you may say [self-direction] is what you want, but when it's offered, it's a little overwhelming.

This reaction underscores Kegan's observation that many self-directed adult programs unwittingly assume that learners have already achieved the level of consciousness they are only beginning to move toward.

As we experience this with our learners, we find we must first create envi-ronments, provide tools, and encourage habits of mind to promote self-direc-tion; we must provide support for the growing edge (Daloz, 1986). If we use self-assessments and journal writing, we encourage a fourth-order capacity for self-reflection; if we use prior learning assessments in the ways described in this volume, we encourage a fourth-order capacity for utilizing and choosing among various frameworks of perception; if we structure group work so that all voices are invited into the conversation, we lay the groundwork for the movement from received to subjective knowing (Belenky, Clinchy, Goldberger, and Tarule, 1986). If we begin with the self and experience and move toward disciplinary frameworks as a means of restructuring that experience, we demonstrate the value of procedural knowing—which is another way of describing fourth-order consciousness.

Conclusion

For a reentry woman, providing she has the courage, tenacity, and support to stay in school, almost any educational program is likely to promote development. Being in an environment where she is seen as an individual and not just as someone's partner or mother (or manager or secretary) helps her define herself that way. Similarly, the sense of accomplishment and confidence that comes with each successfully completed course also leads to greater self-esteem and hence to a clearer sense of self.

Nevertheless, we have tried to show in this volume that some educational practices offer more specific support for developmental growth. Kegan would have it that fourth-order consciousness is a "mental demand of modern life" (1994). The skills needed for effective parenting, partnering, working, healing, dealing with difference, and learning are derived from the fourth-order organizing principles of agency, authority, and autonomy. A result of the shift to the fourth order of consciousness is change, not only in the reentry woman and her immediate community, but also in the wider society of which she is now a more capable member.

Jackie: I started looking at myself and what was going on and in the world around. I just started looking at everything a little differently. . . . Where was I going? What was the point of certain things that I was doing? My job started becoming a real problem too . . . because when you start examining yourself, you examine the whole world around besides yourself. You start going outside.

Kelly: I don't seek change. Now I actively promote change . . . and to call myself an activist, to see myself in that kind of political agenda and want to be in that role, would never have happened had I not had the opportunity to learn about who I am and that I am capable of taking information and making a decision, [and to see] that those things that I'm interested in learning and that I get out of what's going on in the world all point to the same me. So, I am about change.

Gail: So the program became more and more important and the idea of having a degree less important, although that remained the goal. But the process became important. . . . [T]he ultimate example of what a program like this is supposed to do is how it has happened with me. . . . Every task that I set out for myself and that I fulfill—as I'm fulfilling it, I'm becoming . . . [someone] who can live responsibly in a democracy. . . . To live in a democracy, to have a democracy, you have to have people who are not spoon-fed information and then asked to regurgitate the facts, [because then] . . . they can't make decisions concerning who they want to represent them. . . . [Because of] the demands [of self-direction, I'm] able to actively participate . . . in keeping [my] country responsive to the citizenry.

References

Belenky, M. F., Clinchy, B. M., Goldberger, N. R., and Tarule, J. M. *Women's Ways of Knowing: The Development of Self, Voice, and Mind.* New York: Basic Books, 1986.

Caffarella, R. *Psychosocial Development of Women; Linkages to Teaching and Leadership in Adult Education.* Information Series No. 350. Columbus, Ohio: ERIC Clearinghouse on Adult, Career, and Vocational Education, 1992.

Candy, P. C. *Self-Direction for Lifelong Learning: A Comprehensive Guide to Theory and Practice.* San Francisco: Jossey-Bass, 1991.

Daloz, L. A. *Effective Teaching and Mentoring: Realizing the Transformational Power of Adult Learning Experiences.* San Francisco: Jossey-Bass, 1986.

Daloz, L. "The Story of Gladys Who Refused to Grow: A Morality Tale for Mentors." *Lifelong Learning: An Omnibus of Practice & Research,* 1988, *11* (4).

Gilligan, C. *In a Different Voice: Psychological Theory and Women's Development.* Cambridge, Mass.: Harvard University Press, 1982.

Kegan, R. *The Evolving Self: Problem and Process in Human Development.* Cambridge, Mass.: Harvard University Press, 1982.

Kegan, R. *In Over Our Heads: The Mental Demands of Modern Life.* Cambridge, Mass.: Harvard University Press, 1994.

Koller, A. *An Unknown Woman: A Journey to Self-Discovery.* New York: Bantam Books, 1983.

Marienau, C. *Barriers to Adult Participation in Post-Secondary Education as Perceived by Adults in West-Central Minnesota.* Morris: Center for Continuing Education, University of Minnesota at Morris, 1976. (Report.)

Tavris, C. *The Mismeasure of Woman.* New York: Simon & Schuster, 1992.

Taylor, K. "Transforming Learning: Experiences of Adult Development and Transformation of Re-entry Learners in an Adult Degree Program." Unpublished doctoral dissertation, Union Graduate School, The Union Institute, 1991.

KATHLEEN TAYLOR is associate professor at Saint Mary's College of California, chair of the Department of Portfolio Instruction, and a consultant on women's development and education.

CONCLUSION

Much of the literature on teaching methodologies, including those for teaching adults, addresses classroom techniques. This information is useful and may sometimes lead to developmentally supportive practices. However, we have attempted here to more explicitly link teaching to learning and to highlight those strategies that permit and promote developmental growth. Though they may not be aware of or committed to adult development, instructors may assign journals and self-assessments; programs may include a prior learning assessment component; instructors may encourage students to work in groups; and programs may stress self-directed learning. But these and other techniques can be practiced in ways that, although academically sound, are not necessarily developmentally encouraging.

If, as we think likely (and as Kegan [1994] thinks necessary), adult development becomes an increasingly important focus of higher education, we imagine various ways in which institutions may advance this learning outcome. Some may rely on developmental encounters with the right teacher, mentor, or course. Others may expect certain units (for example, student services) or certain courses (for example, women's studies) to carry the developmental flag. We would prefer to see institutions embrace development as part of their mission, to be embodied throughout their practices and dialogues. We hope with this volume to contribute to and advance that goal.

Finally, we wish to clarify two points. First, we acknowledge that, although development is inherently good for any individual, a person's developmental status at any given time is right for that individual at that time. We do not suggest that educators become arbiters of students' developmental progress; rather, we suggest that they seek to build bridges toward change—to meet learners where they are and give them permission and support to journey further.

The propriety of setting goals for students that they might not set for themselves is at the heart of a liberal arts education. Not until someone has sufficient knowledge of this tradition can he or she fully value it. Similarly, only people who have sufficiently advanced along certain developmental continua can perceive the advantages of that development. Just as we wish to encourage increasingly complex thought and expression in our students as they progress through college, we might appropriately wish to encourage in them increasingly complex developmental perspectives. For that matter, the two are likely related (Haswell, 1991).

Second, in describing the vulnerabilities of reentry women, we have not intended to present them as only being fragile, overanxious, or weak—we know them to have a full range of qualities, including being powerful, indomitable, and successful. But perhaps the images most deeply etched for us are of those women who succeeded despite formidable odds or those whose growth was especially memorable in light of where they started from. And perhaps as developing women ourselves, with histories and journeys of our own, we are most attached to stories that remind us of our own struggles, strengths, growth, and change.

As we continue to learn from our learners, from our reflections on our practice, and from theory, we are confident that the repertoire of support for learning and development will grow in effectiveness and in kind. "Who comes into a person's life may be the single greatest factor of influence to what that life becomes," says Kegan (1982, p. 19). We wish in the future to come into our learners' lives as they have into ours, bringing gifts of awareness, caring, and the potential for lifelong growth.

Kathleen Taylor
Catherine Marienau
Editors

References

Haswell, R. *Gaining Ground in College Writing: Tales of Development and Interpretation.* Dallas, Tex.: Southern Methodist University Press, 1991.

Kegan, R. *The Evolving Self: Problem and Process in Human Development.* Cambridge, Mass.: Harvard University Press, 1982.

Kegan, R. *In Over Our Heads: The Mental Demands of Modern Life.* Cambridge, Mass.: Harvard University Press, 1994.

INDEX

Academic language, 47, 50, 55; PLA and, 29–30, 34–35
Acceptance, self, 39–40
Adams, K., 14
Adult development: core curriculum for, 53–54, 57–60; education's role in, 11, 25–26, 34, 38–41, 48–51, 76, 93–94; ethical concerns in fostering, 80–81; Kegan's constructive model of, 10, 84–87, 90; learning-centered pedagogy and, 77–80; and meaning making, 21–22, 75–77
Adult development theories: chronological-stage, 17; female-centered, 42–43, 60; teaching, 19; women's experience and, 7–10
Adult learning theory, 34, 78
African American women, 5–6, 26, 45–46, 83–84
Age of learners, 6, 38, 57, 60, 75
Alternative adult higher education, 7, 42
American Association of University Women (AAUW), 57–58
Applebee, A., 49
Appreciative thinking, 56
Apprenticeship, 78, 79
Assessment. *See* Prior learning assessment
At a Journal Workshop, 16–17
Autobiographies, 30. *See also* Journal writing

Barriers, institutional, 7, 31
Beginnings and endings, writing of, 15
Belenky, M. F., 1, 8–10, 11, 17, 23, 24, 25, 26, 30, 31, 32, 38, 41, 45, 47, 48, 50, 54–60, 66, 69, 90
Black vernacular English (BVE), 46
Bloom, M., 70
Bridges, W., 15, 23

Caffarella, R., 8, 42, 75, 87
Canale, M., 47
Candy, P. C., 89
Caring by mentors, 63, 67–68, 70, 71
Carlsen, M. B., 75
Carnegie Commission on Higher Education, 7
Carson, J., 47–48

Changes, making, 41, 81, 83–84; in perspectives, 40, 42–43, 91. *See also* Transitions
Chickering, A. W., 8
Chinese students, 47–48
Chodorow, N., 8
Choices, recognizing, 24, 25, 41
Chronological record, portfolio, 30
Clark, M. C., 77
Clinchy, B. M., 1, 8–10, 11, 17, 23, 24, 25, 26, 30, 31, 32, 38, 41, 45, 47, 48, 50, 54–60, 66, 69, 90
"College Enrollment by Age of Students, Fall 1992," 6
Communication competence, 47
Connected procedural knowing, 55–56, 69
Connection, 40, 74
Consciousness: five orders of, 10, 22, 84–87; third-order, 10, 32, 50, 84–85. *See also* Fourth-order consciousness
Constructed knowing, 9, 56–57, 59–60
Conversation, 65–71, 74
Cooperation vs. competition, 58
Credit. *See* Prior learning assessment
Critical thinking, 50, 55
Cross, K. P., 7
Culminating Seminar courses, 59–60
Culture: and reality, 47; world, 58–59
Curriculum for adult women learners, 53–54, 57–60

Daloz, L. A., 27, 63, 64, 65–66, 87–88, 90
Danison, N., 47–48
Darrow, C., 17, 18, 42
Democracy, 91
Development. *See* Adult development
Developmental (cognitive) model of teaching, 78, 79
Developmental studies, 46–47, 49–50
Dialogues, journal, 17–18
Dinnerstein, D., 8
Diversity: of educational aims, 80, 93; exposure to, 58–59; of nonmainstream learners, 45–52
Divorced women, 6, 32, 83–84

Education: ethical concerns on, 80–81;

95

Women of color, 5–6, 26, 38, 45–46, 47–48, 83–84
Women undergraduates, number of, 6
Women's development. *See* Adult development
Women's feelings. *See* Feelings of women learners
Women's Psychosocial Development course, 37, 41–43

Women's Ways of Knowing, 8–10, 23, 24, 41, 54–57, 60, 69
Writing: experiential learning essays, 31–33; journals, 14–19; with a mentor, 70; in a second language, 46, 49–50

Zencey, E., 34
Zone of proximal development, 70

Ordering Information

NEW DIRECTIONS FOR ADULT AND CONTINUING EDUCATION is a series of paperback books that explores issues of common interest to instructors, administrators, counselors, and policy makers in a broad range of adult and continuing education settings—such as colleges and universities, extension programs, businesses, the military, prisons, libraries, and museums. Books in the series are published quarterly in Spring, Summer, Fall, and Winter and are available for purchase by subscription and individually.

SUBSCRIPTIONS for 1995 cost $48.00 for individuals (a savings of 25 percent over single-copy prices) and $64.00 for institutions, agencies, and libraries. Please do not send institutional checks for personal subscriptions. Standing orders are accepted.

SINGLE COPIES cost $16.95 when payment accompanies order. (California, New Jersey, New York, and Washington, D.C., residents please include appropriate sales tax.) All orders will be charged shipping and handling.

DISCOUNTS FOR QUANTITY ORDERS are available. Please write to the address below for information.

ALL ORDERS must include either the name of an individual or an official purchase order number. Please submit your order as follows:
    Subscriptions: specify series and year subscription is to begin
    Single copies: include individual title code (such as ACE 59)

MAIL ALL ORDERS TO:
    Jossey-Bass Publishers
    350 Sansome Street
    San Francisco, California 94104-1342

FOR SUBSCRIPTION SALES OUTSIDE OF THE UNITED STATES, contact any international subscription agency or Jossey-Bass directly.